# Rugmaking:
# 3 Quick
# and Easy Ways

# Rugmaking: 3 Quick and Easy Ways

## JOAN SCOBEY & MARJORIE SABLOW

Bobbs-Merrill

INDIANAPOLIS / NEW YORK

Published by The Bobbs-Merrill Company, Inc.
Indianapolis / New York

Library of Congress Cataloging in Publication Data
Scobey, Joan.
   Rugmaking: 3 Quick and Easy Ways

   1. Rugs.   I. Sablow, Marjorie, joint author.   II. Title.
TT850.S2      746.7'4      76-26768
ISBN 0-672-52132-6

Designed by Tom Torre Bevans
Manufactured in the United States of America
First printing

*To Rick who punched "Mount Fuji and Great Waves"*

*And Jennifer who made the doll hanging*

*And Wendy who latched the lion*

*And David who carried the banner*

# CONTENTS

# Introduction

*The making of rugs often seems a grand and complicated art. Perhaps it is the scale of the project that overwhelms, perhaps imagined intricacies of design, or mysteries of the rugmaking techniques—but surely, it is thought, no place for a novice to try one's hand.*

*Nothing could be further from the truth; the association of novices and rugmaking is long and honorable.*

*In earlier times, rugs were a basic necessity for survival, so everyone—beginners and more accomplished craftsmen both—was expected to contribute to their manufacture. Rugs were hung over doors and windows to keep out wind and cold; laid on the ground to give some measure of warmth and comfort underfoot. They provided insulation against heat as well as cold. And when people moved from place to place, their rugs literally became carpet bags to transport their worldly goods.*

*Because rugs were an essential part of everyday life, making them was an essential skill, passed on from one generation to the next, continually schooling beginners in the craft and creating an intimate bond between people and the textiles they needed and produced. As life grew more sophisticated, rugs began to take on a more decorative role. Central heating and wall insulation usurped their prime utilitarian function, so it was no longer necessary for households to train their own rugmakers.*

*With the increasing importance of the ornamental value, the craft of making rugs and tapestries was left to artisans and artists; novices, unless they became apprentices to guild masters, no longer had a craft relationship with the textiles that decorated their floors and walls. The Industrial Revolution altered this relationship still further, and even the textile artisans lost their close identity with their product. Rugs and carpets had entered the province of technology, and clearly there was no place for a beginning craftsman.*

*Happily this is changing, for we again value the hand-crafted, the unique, the special rug that cannot be made by machine. And from the technology of rugmaking, artisans have adapted more efficient hand tools, better and more uniform quality of yarns. Our textile artists have regained their importance in the marketplace, and begin-*

ning rugmakers now search out teachers who can transmit the ancient skills of rugmaking, refined with contemporary methods.

It is in this spirit that we offer this book. It contains simple, straightforward instructions for making rugs by three basic methods: latch hooking to produce a shaggy texture; needlepoint for the flat look; punch hooking for a looped surface. These three techniques are all large-stitch methods that cover the backing material quickly and give almost instant satisfaction and pleasure to impatient neophytes.

In addition to the instructions and illustrative line drawings for each rugmaking technique, the book offers thirty-one widely varied designs, each presented in full color in three different color schemes. Every design can be made in all of our rugmaking methods. In keeping with the nature of the book, none of the rugs requires joins, complicated maneuvers, or difficult finishing techniques. But the boldness and effectiveness of the designs belie their ease of execution in any technique you choose.

It is our hope that this book will instill appreciation for an old and honored craft. And that as beginners you will learn and master the basic tools and techniques, quickly becoming artisans of this gratifying and pleasurable art form.

# PART ONE

# The Rug Designs

# All About the Rug Designs

On pages 25-55 you will find designs for thirty-one rugs. Some will beguile nature lovers, whether they favor animals, birds, flowers, or just mushrooms. Some are for sports fans, for car buffs, for music lovers. There are Chinese and Persian motifs for oriental rug afficionados, and abstract and pop designs that defy classification.

## THE COLOR COLLECTION

Each rug design is presented in three different color schemes, plus a monochrome version.

They're shown in a color collection on pages 17-24, so you can see how they look in a variety of colorways. You may want to choose one that complements an existing color scheme in your home, or you may simply be charmed by the fanciful notion of a blue lion or a pink sun. You may prefer to work out your own scheme by combining tones from two or three of the choices, or selecting entirely original colors.

In addition, you'll use the color gallery as a guide when you're actually stitching your rug.

All the designs are appropriate for neophyte rugmakers, combining simplicity of line with design interest. And all of them are workable in any of the three rugmaking techniques—latch hook, needlepoint, and punch hook—all fully described in Part II.

## THE WORKING DESIGNS

Once you've chosen a design, refer to its "working design," pages 25-55, same order as in the "color collection." This is an enlarged replica in which colors are defined by five different shades of gray plus black and white. Some working designs will use all the grays plus black and white to denote a total of seven colors; others use just a few. You will use the working design to enlarge your design into an actual rug-size pattern. Complete instructions for doing this are explained in the chapter entitled "Enlarging the Designs."

Now, browse through the color collection and see which one catches your fancy.

Design 3

Design 4

Design 1

Design 2

17

Design 5

Design 6

Design 10

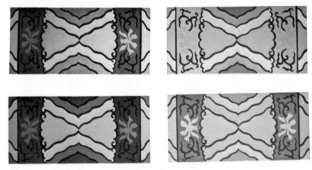

Design 7

Design 11

Design 8

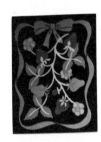

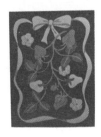

Design 12

Design 9

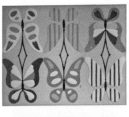
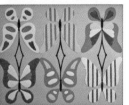
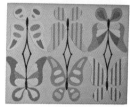

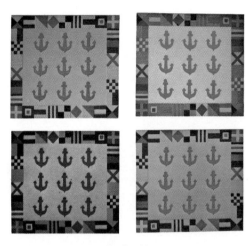

Design 16

Design 13

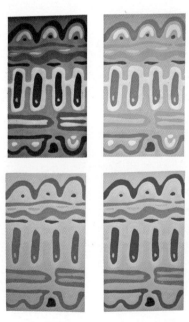

Design 14

Design 17

19

Design 15

Design 18

Design 19

Design 20

Design 21

Design 22

Design 23

Design 24

Design 25

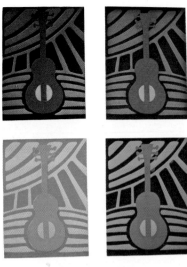

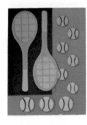

Design 26

Design 29

Design 27

Design 30

Design 28

Design 31

21

Floral rug (Design 1) shown in
three techniques.
TOP: needlepoint.
BOTTOM LEFT: a section in punch hooking.
BOTTOM RIGHT: a section in latch hooking.

22

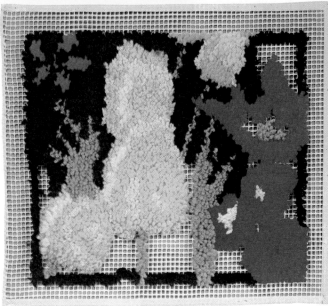

Lions (Design 6), latch hooked for a shaggy look

Mount Fuji and Great Waves (Design 9),
punch hooked for a loopy look

24

Design 2

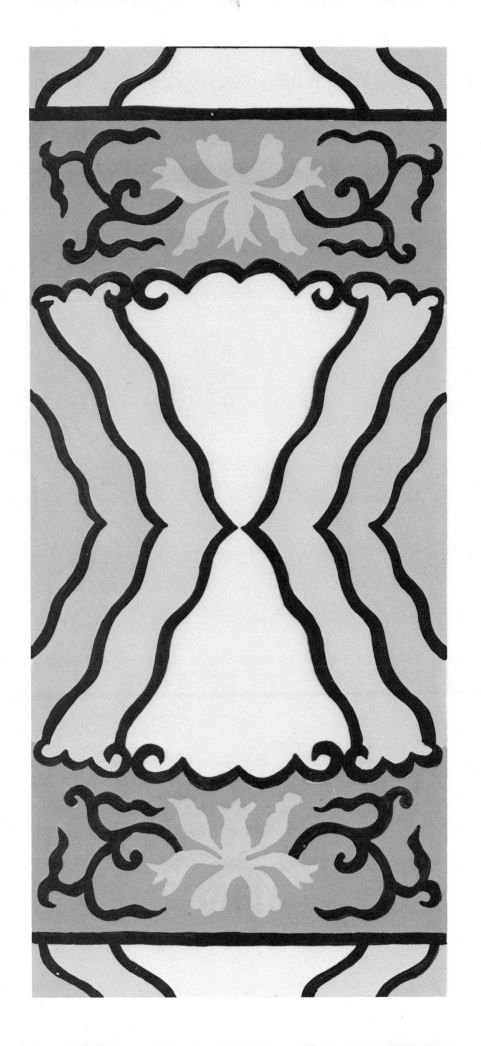

Design 14

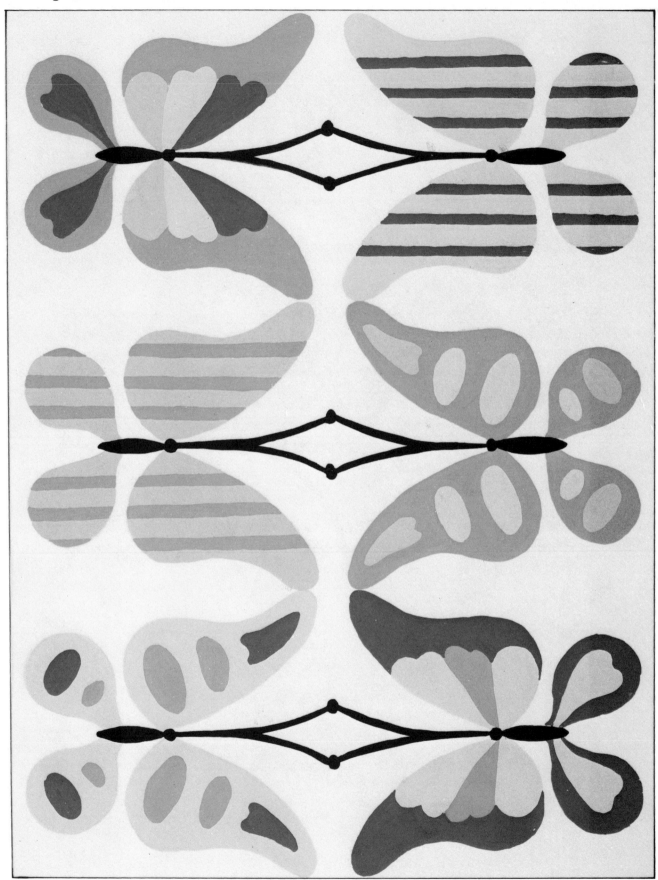

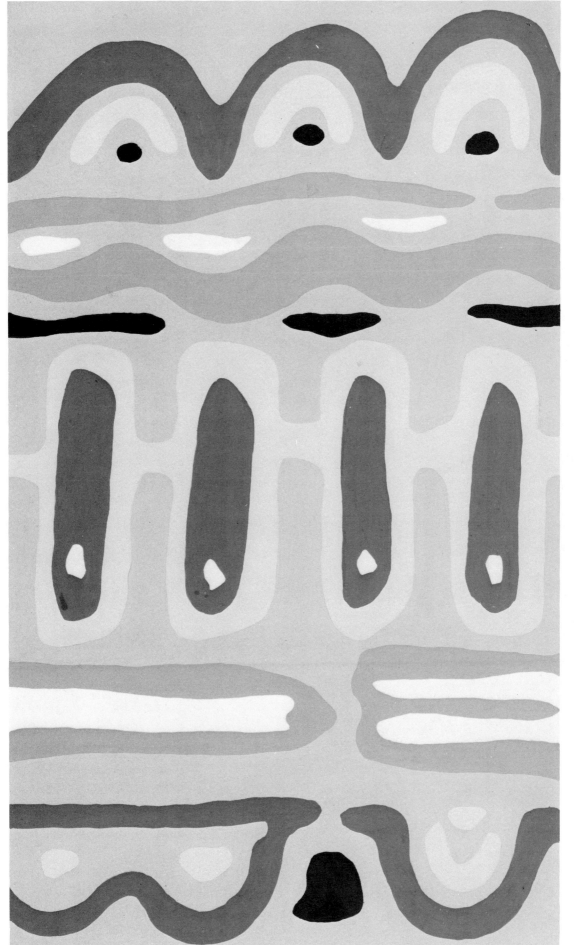

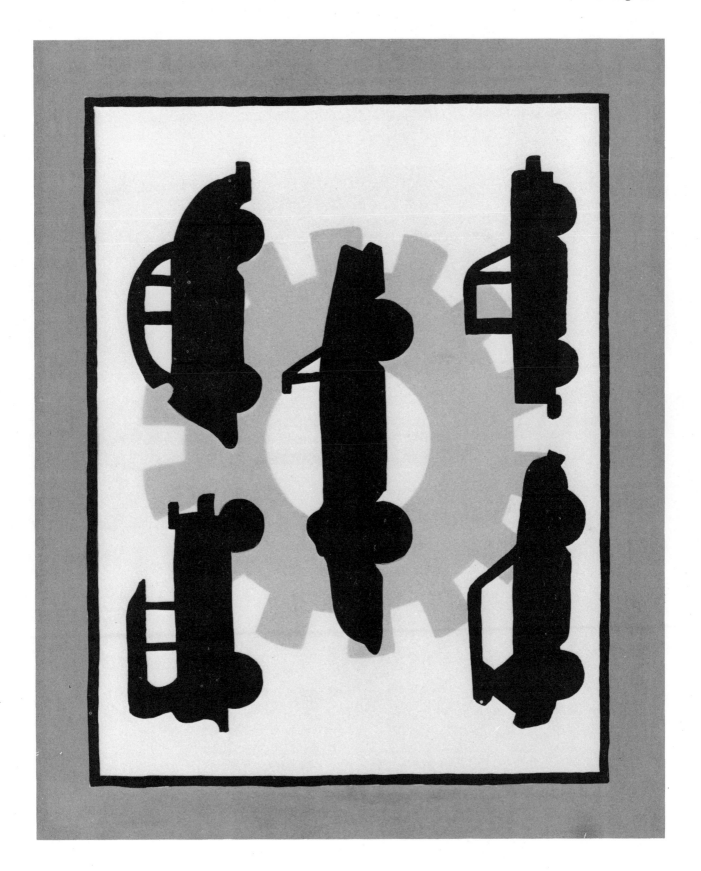

Design 22

BEWARE OF DOG

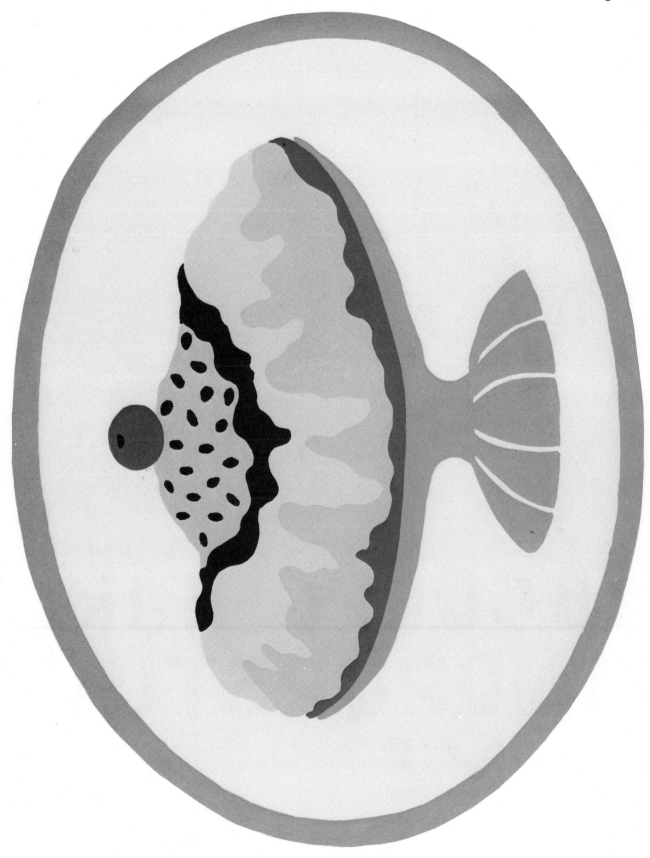

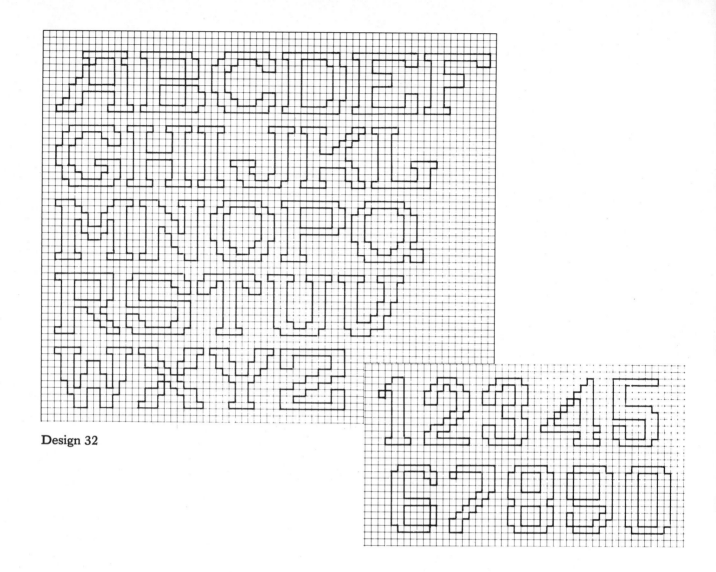

Design 32

# ABCDEFGHIJKL
# MNOPQRSTUV
# WXYZ
# 1234567890

Design 33

# Enlarging the Designs

When you have selected the rug you want to make, turn to its working design—that is, the enlarged replica painted in black and white and shades of gray. Lay a sheet of tracing paper over the book page and on it trace the working design, including the perimeter (see Fig. 1). You now have a line drawing ready to be enlarged to the size of your finished rug.

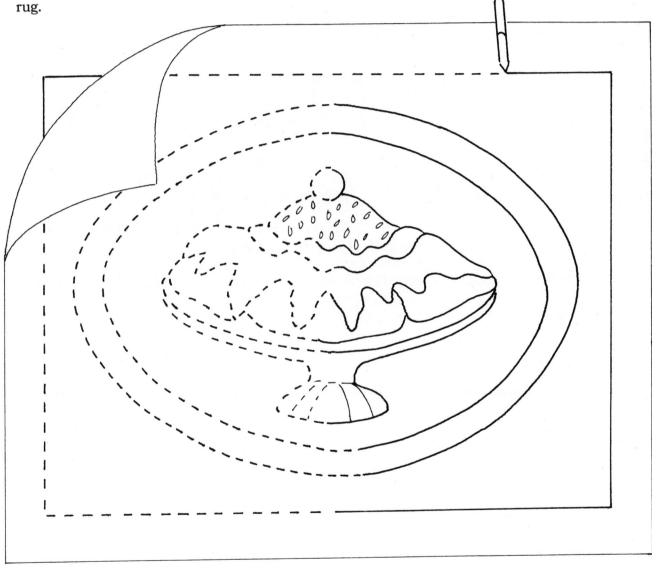

Fig. 1

There are two ways to enlarge your drawing: by photostat or by the box method. Photostating is easier and more accurate, but it can be costly, especially if you want a fairly large rug.

## PHOTOSTAT METHOD

Photostating is a professional service which can be located in the classified pages of your telephone book under Photo Copying or Blueprinting. Photostating will enlarge the drawing—the overall shape and exterior boundaries of the rug as well as the design—to any size you desire without changing its proportions. Some firms can make enlargements up to 54 by 170 inches; others will piece together smaller photostats to get an outsize enlargement. Order a "positive" photostat—black lines on a white background—or you will probably receive a negative, which has white lines on a black background. The positive may cost more, but it is much easier to work with.

You will use this life-size rug pattern to put your design on the rug backing, as described in Part II under each of the various rugmaking techniques.

## BOX METHOD

The alternate way to enlarge your drawing is by the box method. For this you first establish the overall size of your finished rug and mark that life-size shape on a piece of sturdy paper sufficiently large to accommodate it; brown wrapping paper is excellent for this purpose. The various rug shapes are enlarged as follows:

*A rectangle or square:* On two adjacent sides of the blank wrapping paper rule perpendicular lines; these will represent the left side and bottom of your full-size rug. To establish the right side, mark the desired width of your rug on the bottom line and draw the right side straight up from that mark, parallel to the left (see Fig. 2).

Fig. 2

Place your traced line drawing over the brown paper in the left corner, matching its bottom line and left side with the lines drawn on the wrapping paper. (Hold it accurately in place with tacks or tape.) Lay a yardstick or piece of string diagonally across the tracing from its lower left corner through the upper right corner, and mark the point at which it crosses the right side line on the wrapping paper (see Fig. 3). Connect this point with the left side line to complete your enlarged rectangle or square (see Fig. 4).

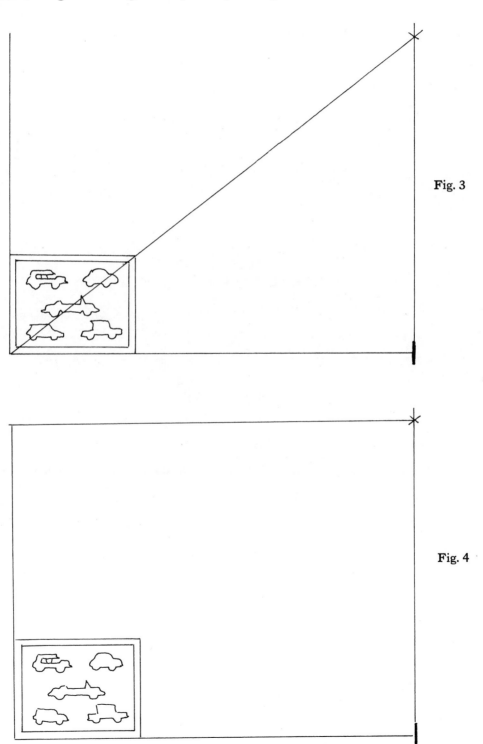

Fig. 3

Fig. 4

*An oval or irregular shape:* Enclose the traced oval or irregular shape in a rectangle (see Fig. 5) and enlarge that rectangle as described above. The size of the rectangle doesn't matter; it is used only as a vehicle in the enlargement process.

Fig. 5

*A circle:* On the piece of blank wrapping paper, find the center by folding it in half, then in half again. Lay the paper on a wooden board and tack the point of a thin nail in it at the center point.

Measure the radius (half the diameter) of the finished circle, and cut a piece of thin picture wire two inches longer; that is, if you want a rug 36 inches in diameter, cut the wire 20 inches long (18 inches plus two extra inches). Wind one inch of wire at one end around the center nail and wind an inch of wire at the other end around a marking pen. Holding the marker vertical, draw a circle on the paper (see Fig. 6).

*A semicircle:* Draw a horizontal line across the bottom of the blank wrapping paper. To outline the half circle, follow the procedure described above for a circle but, instead of tacking the nail into the center of the paper, tack it into the center of the horizontal line. Draw the semicircle by swinging the marking pen and wire in an arc from one side of the line to the other (see Fig. 7).

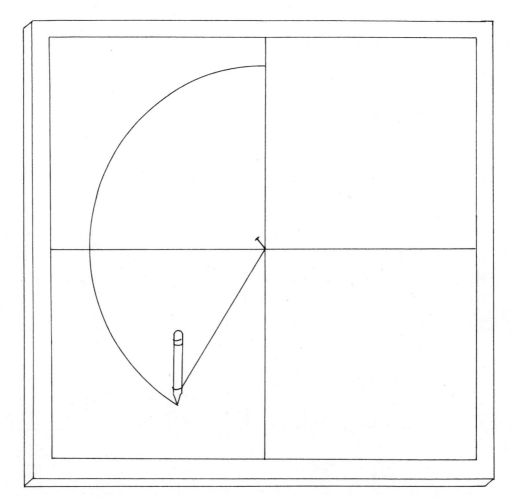

Fig. 6

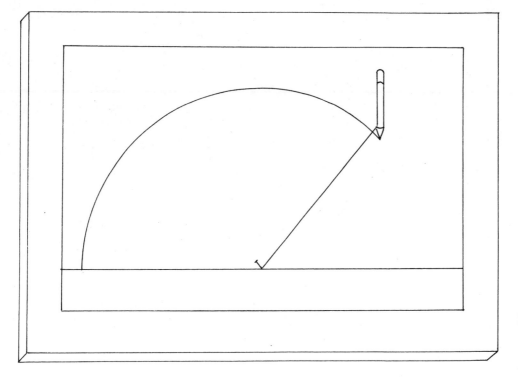

Fig. 7

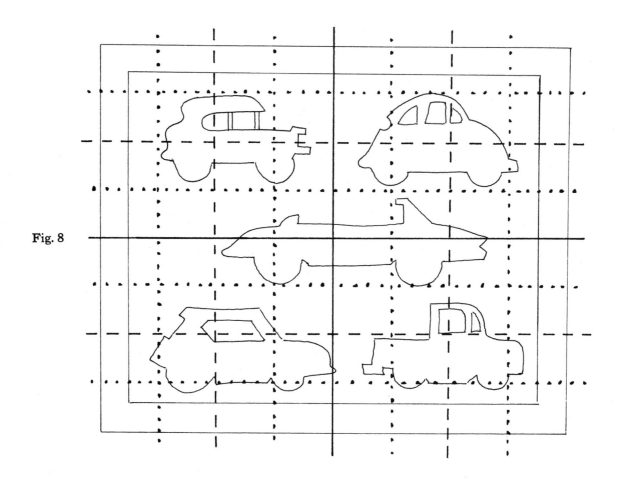

Fig. 8

With the overall shape of your finished project outlined on the large piece of wrapping paper, you can now
transfer the design by the box method, following these
steps:

1. Establish a grid of small boxes over the traced
line drawing (see Figs. 8, 9, and 10) by marking lines
across the center of the drawing, both horizontally and vertically (the unbroken lines), then dividing each quarter
into its own smaller quarters (the broken lines), then sub-
dividing those boxes into still smaller boxes (the dotted
lines). In this way you create a grid over the entire drawing,
whether the shape of the rug is rectangular, oval, circular,
or semicircular.

2. Now draw a corresponding grid on your outlined
brown wrapping paper, dividing it in the same way (see

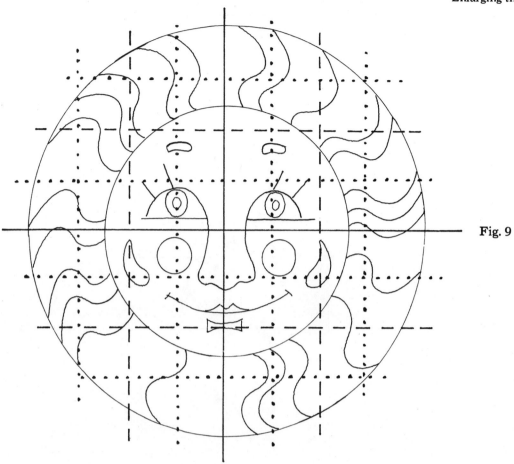

Fig. 9

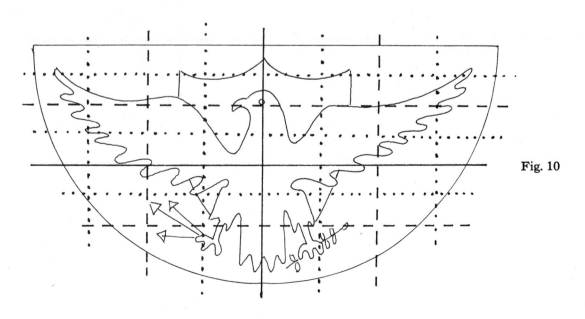

Fig. 10

Fig. 11). As you see, the enlarged outline contains the same number of boxes in exactly the same configuration as the traced drawing; only their size is different.

3. Now transfer the design from the traced drawing onto the brown paper, copying the lines contained in each small box of the traced drawing into its corresponding box, working freehand, box by box, until the entire design is transferred (see Fig. 12). When you enlarge an oval or irregular-shaped rug, its outline will be transferred along with its design (see Fig. 13).

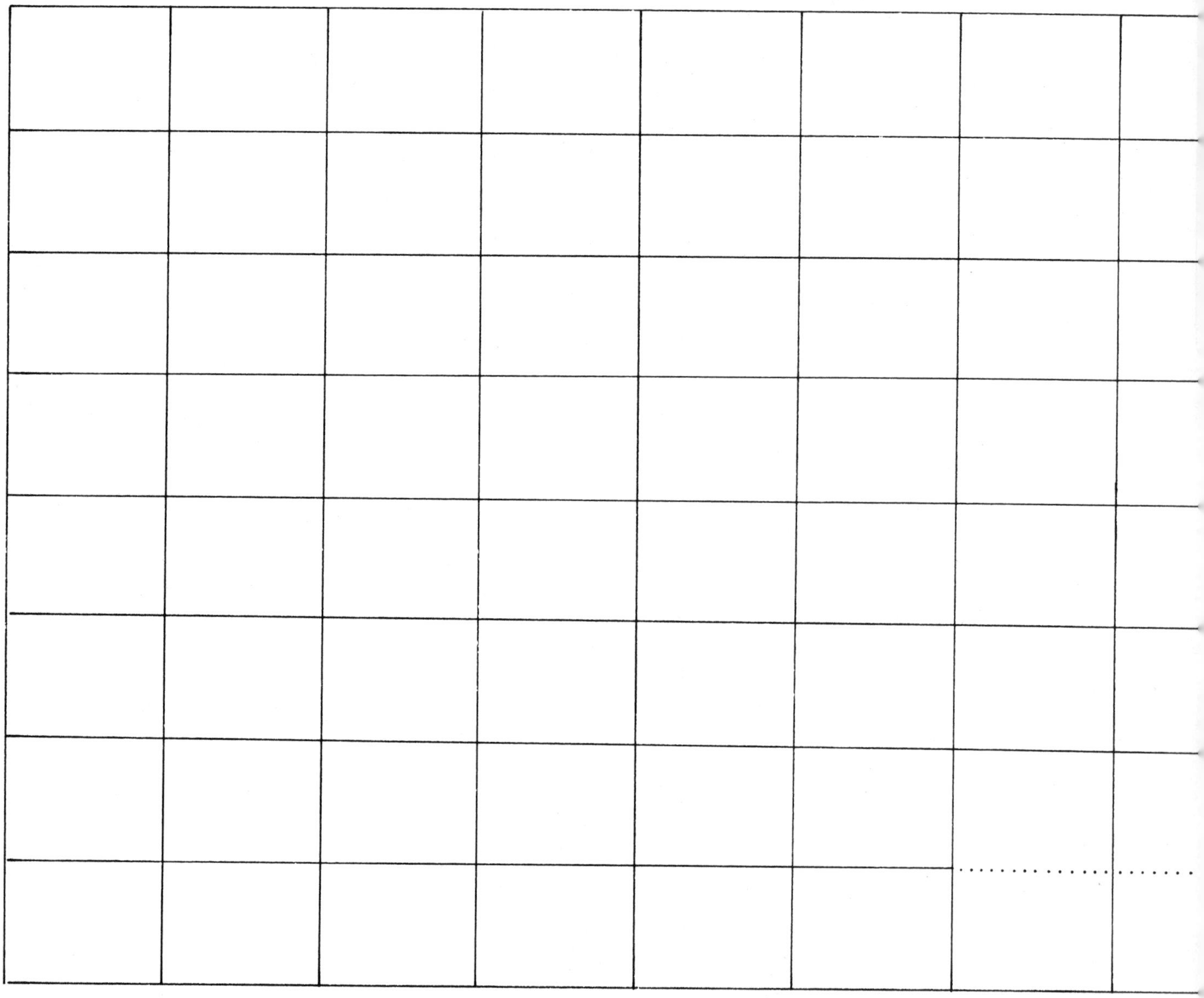

Fig. 11

Finally, go over your design so it stands out in bold dark lines. A black waterproof marker is good for this.

Note: If you are planning a very large rug and find that the boxes on the enlarged outline are too big to transfer the design accurately enough, just subdivide both grids still further, making sure that both sets of boxes correspond in number and location.

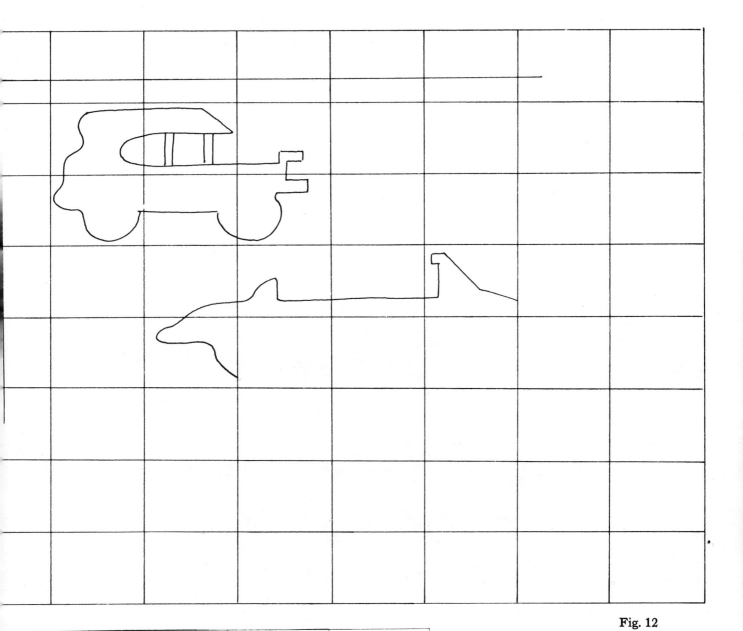

Fig. 12

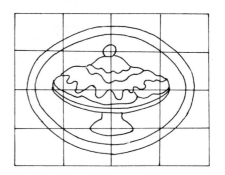

Fig. 13

65

# WORKING WITH LETTERS AND NUMBERS

Two sets of alphabets and numbers are offered in the preceding design section. The "cloud" set is particularly appropriate for punch hooking because its fluid lines are nicely translated by the punch hooking technique (fully explained in Part II). The "block" set is suited to latch hooking and needlepoint because its "stepped" outlines are easily adapted to the grid of their canvas mesh. The block alphabet can also be used in punch hooking; in that case, you may want to smooth over the stepped outline (see Fig. 14).

Fig. 14

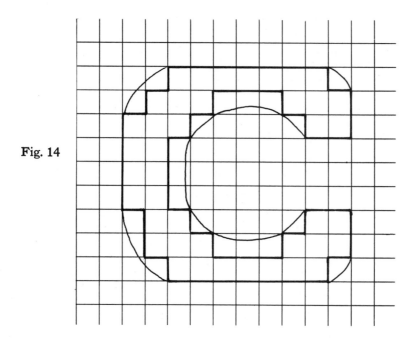

For punch hooking, trace the outline of the letters or numbers as you would any other design element, then enlarge to the desired size by photostating or by the box method (see Fig. 15). Place the enlarged letters or numbers in position on the brown paper pattern, aligned and evenly spaced, and glue them down (see Fig. 16). Now the entire design, including the letters or numbers, is ready to be put on the rug backing, a process fully described with the punch-hooking technique in Part II.

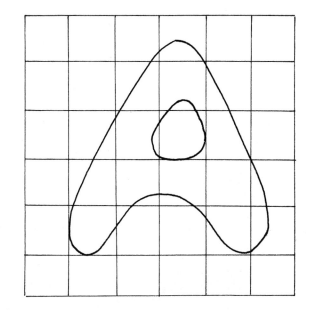

Fig. 15

Fig. 16

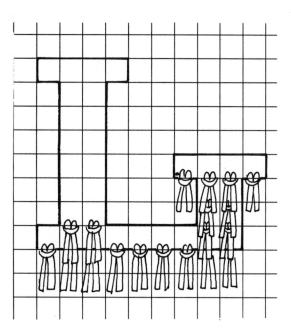

Fig. 17

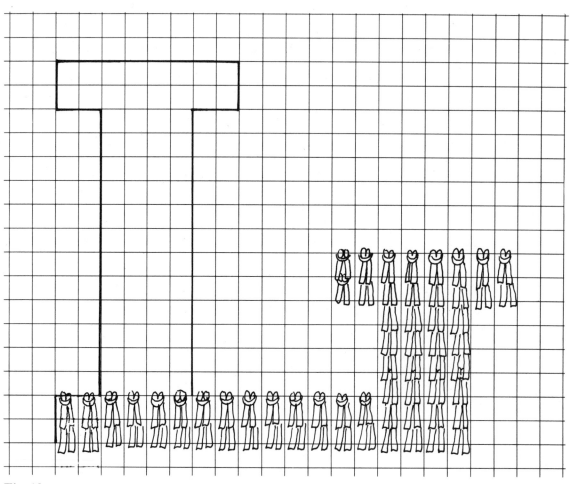

Fig. 18

Fig. 19

Because of the nature of latch hooking and needle-point (also explained in Part II), each letter or number is designated not by its outline but by the number of boxes *within* that outline. In latch hooking, each box represents one mesh of latch hooking canvas, and hence one stitch made in that mesh (see Fig. 17). In needlepoint, each box designates one intersection of the needlepoint canvas, and hence one stitch made across that intersection; arbitrarily, make that stitch in the upper right corner of the box (see Fig. 18).

In latch hooking and needlepoint, block letters and numbers cannot be enlarged by the box method or by photostating; they can only be enlarged by letting each square within the figure stand for more than one stitch. An enlarged letter "L," for example, will have double the number of stitches as boxes, or triple the number of stitches as boxes (see Figs. 19 and 20).

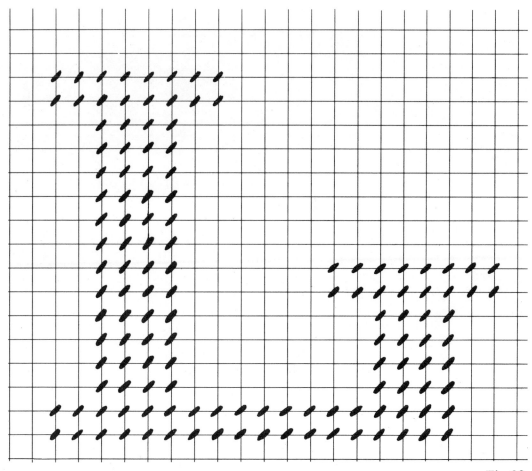

Fig. 20

Whenever you use letters or numbers, position them accurately, space them evenly, and align them carefully. If you want to make a school banner, for instance, it will be helpful if you first make the rug-size outline and locate the center. Then work from the center out and space the letters evenly (see Fig. 21).

In a similar manner, initial your rug in a corner if you like. Your rug-size paper pattern should include all the desired lettering in addition to the design, and then you will be ready to turn to the actual rugmaking.

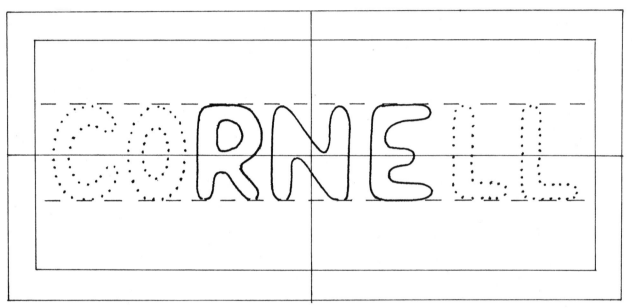

Fig. 21

# PART TWO

# The Rugmaking & Finishing Techniques

# *Which Rugmaking Technique to Choose*

The three rugmaking methods we suggest for beginners are latch hooking, needlepoint, and punch hooking. Each of them produces a different "look" and texture; each has its own advantages and disadvantages. All of them are eminently suited to all of our rug designs.

Study the characteristics and techniques of each rugmaking method and you will probably find one with special appeal, thus dictating your choice of technique. Indeed, you may even find that their varying distinctions will commend them all, and you will want to try each in turn.

Latch hooking is the way to produce a soft velvety texture and deep pile. A luxuriant pile of uniform height is formed by knotting precut lengths of yarn into a canvas rug backing with a special tool. The special latch hook and the precut yarns assure the uniformity of the stitches, rewarding a beginner with the same consistent success as an accomplished rugmaker. This happy and unique characteristic makes possible a joint stitching project with a friend or family member, since too many hands can't spoil the cloth with uneven stitches. Moreover, latch hooking proceeds quickly, causing designs to spring to life at a fairly rapid pace which is especially pleasing to a beginner.

LATCH HOOKING

Fig. 22

73

Needlepoint is the technique of choice if you want a flat look with maximum detail of design. Needlepoint rugs, once the exclusive province of advanced and devoted stitchers with time and patience to work a large area of small-mesh canvas, are now attractive to beginners, primarily because of the development of a perfected large-mesh needlepoint canvas admirably suited to rugmaking. Although a needlepoint rug takes more time to stitch than one in latch hooking or punch hooking, it offers compensatory qualities: it is more easily portable, its yarns are available in a wide range of glorious colors and shades, and it allows for greater detail in the design because of the relatively smaller size of the canvas mesh.

NEEDLEPOINT

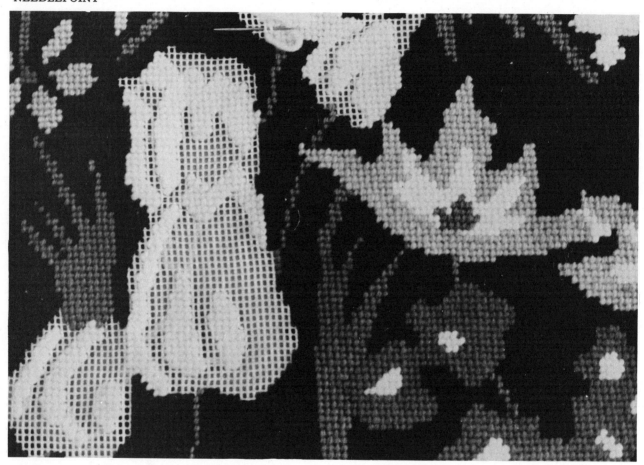

Fig. 23

Punch hooking creates a looped pebbly texture, the familiar look of early American hooked rugs. While the rugs of our forefathers were originally made by pulling strips of cloth through a backing material with a bent nail, contemporary techniques have made the process easier and faster. A special punching tool replaces the bent nail, and spun yarns substitute for the tedious process of cutting fabric strips—improvements which commend punch hooking to the neophyte.

Also beguiling to the beginner is the pictorial accuracy possible in a punch-hooked rug. Not confined by the rigid grid of latch-hooking and needlepoint canvas, the punch hooker can roam over the rug backing in large free strokes to duplicate undulating waves and curves with his needle, then turn in a tight circle to fill in a small free-form detail. A variety of surface textures is possible as well, since many punch hookers can form loops of varying heights with a simple mechanical adjustment of the tool. Rug yarn, skeins of needlepoint yarn, knitting yarn—all are suitable to one or more of the various punch hook needles, considerably enlarging the choices of yarns and colors.

The most serious disadvantage of punch hooking is

PUNCH HOOKING

Fig. 24

the frame over which the rug backing must be stretched for stitching. This cumbersome arrangement effectively restricts punch hooking to the home, since the frame can't be carried around easily.

Before settling on a technique for your first rug, read the following three chapters carefully. They describe in full the techniques and tools for latch hooking, needlepoint, and punch hooking, and these may also influence your choice of rugmaking method.

# Latch It
# For a Shaggy Look

Fig. 25

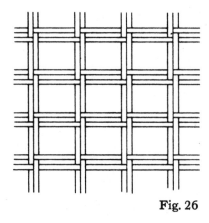

Fig. 26

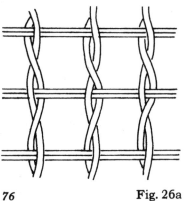

## TOOLS OF THE TRADE

To make a latch-hooked rug or wall hanging you will need the following equipment:

canvas
masking tape
latch hook
precut yarn

### Canvas

Latch-hook canvas is coarsely woven, usually of white cotton, with anywhere from 3½ to 4 holes per inch, depending on the manufacturer. It may have two clearly defined threads running both horizontally and vertically, as in Fig. 26. Or its threads may be more closely paired, with the vertical threads twisted, as in Fig. 26a. Either type of canvas is designed for latch hooking.

With the selvage of the material running vertically, cut the canvas two inches larger on all sides than your design. Bind the cut edges with masking tape to prevent raveling (see Fig. 27).

Fig. 26a

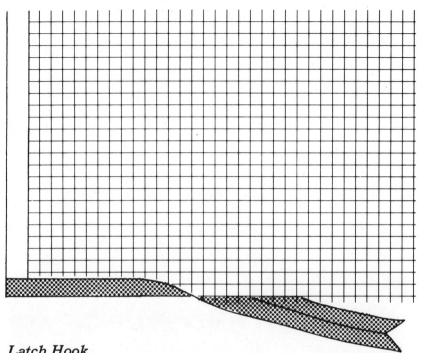

Fig. 27

## Latch Hook

All latch hooks are designed with the same features: a handle, shaft, curved hook, and a moving latch that locks each stitch in place in the canvas (see Fig. 28). They are all used with precut pieces of yarn of virtually any thickness and length.

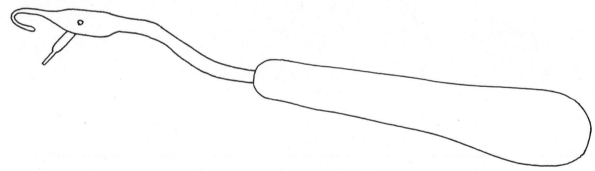

## Yarn

Precut rug yarn is made by different manufacturers in anywhere from 36 to about 60 colors. It is sold in one-ounce packages, each containing between 320 and 360 pieces of yarn; each piece is usually 2 to 2½ inches long and has 4 to 6 plies twisted together. Since differences in weight and length among the various brands are negligible, you can use precut rug yarns interchangeably, thus enlarging your choice of colors. At most, you may have to trim back a few slightly longer ends to even the pile after you have finished hooking.

If you need a color that is not available in precut yarn, buy it in a skein of comparable weight and cut lengths of yarn as you need them. An easy way to cut a number of pieces at one time is to wind the yarn in a single layer

Fig. 28

around a stiff piece of cardboard measuring half the needed length, then cut the yarn through the middle (see Fig. 29). (Winding yarn in a single layer will keep the pieces a uniform length.) Art needlework shops carry commercial yarn gauges which can produce pieces from 3 to 7 inches long.

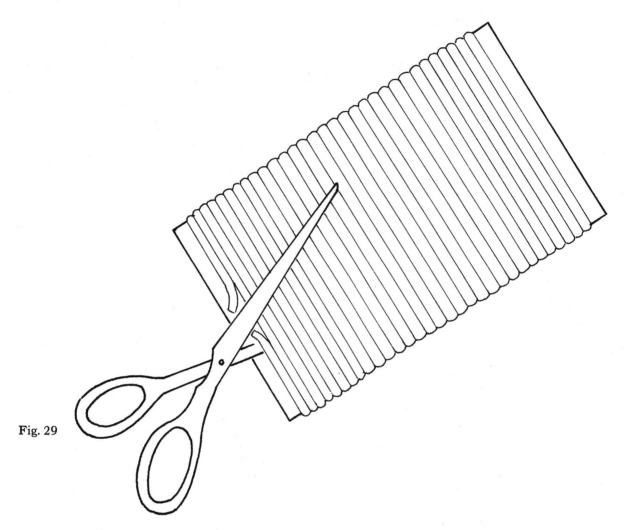

Fig. 29

\*\*\* If you plan to finish your project with tassels or a fringe, buy an uncut skein of yarn in a color and weight to match your precut yarn.

\*\*\* If you like the shaggier look of rya rugs, use a rya-type yarn now available in tightly twisted, longer precut lengths simulating the length and texture of Scandinavian rya yarn. Use it with the latch hook in the same way as with the regular precut yarns, using the instructions which follow.

*Estimating your yarn needs.* Since each stitch requires one piece of precut yarn, you can figure your yarn requirements fairly closely.

1. Determine the coverage of one package of the yarn you are using on your canvas. For example, brand A

contains 360 pieces of precut yarn. On a canvas with 4 mesh—and stitches—to the inch and 16 mesh—and stitches —to the square inch, one full package of brand A will cover 22½ square inches. Brand B contains 320 pieces of yarn; used on the same canvas, one package of brand B would cover 20 square inches.

2. Figure out the number of square inches in your project. For example, a rug measuring 2 by 4 feet contains 1,152 square inches.

3. Divide the area of your rug by the coverage of your yarn on the rug canvas you are using (as computed in Step 1). For instance, if you are using brand A on 4-mesh-to-the-inch canvas, you will need a total of 51.2 ounces, or 52 packages of yarn (1,152 divided by 22½). If you are using brand B on the same canvas, you will need 57.6 ounces, or 58 packages of yarn (1,152 divided by 20).

4. If you are using two or three colors, divide the total yarn requirements proportionately among them. However, if you are using a number of different colors, you should compute the yarn needs individually. First estimate the area of each color in square inches, then divide by the coverage of your brand yarn, as computed above. To determine the background area, add up the total area covered by the design, subtract it from the total area of the rug, and translate it into packages of yarn using the same formula. As you will see, the more colors you use, the higher your total yarn needs will be; there will be some loss of coverage since you will probably be left with partially used packages as you change colors.

\*\*\* Buy generous amounts of yarn in the same dye lots; unopened packages are usually returnable.

\*\*\* If your yarn lists its contents by weight rather than by number of yarn pieces, you can safely figure that one ounce of regular precut latch hook yarn will cover about 20 inches on any rug-size canvas mesh.

## GETTING READY TO WORK

### Putting the Design on the Backing

With your life-size design in hand (as described in the chapter on "Enlarging the Designs"), you are ready to transfer it to your prepared rug canvas.

1. Be sure the enlarged design is outlined in bold dark lines. If any of the lines are fuzzy or indistinct, go over them with a black waterproof marker.

2. Lay the enlarged design face up, and over it position the rug canvas with the selvage running up and down. Tape them together. The darkened lines of the design should be clearly visible through the rug canvas, but if you want even more visibility, work on a white table top or on the floor over a white sheet.

3. Trace the design onto the rug canvas with a waterproof marker (see Fig. 30). This marker need not be black; in fact, it should not be dark in areas of light color, but it must be waterproof.

Fig. 30

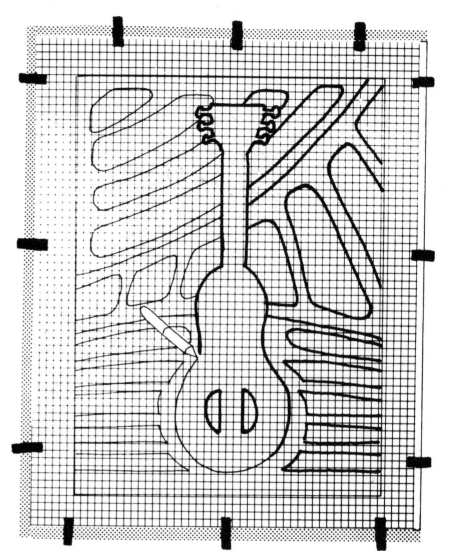

Fig. 31

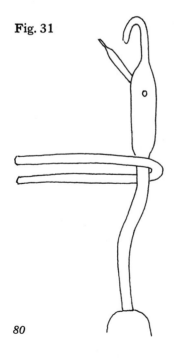

4. For color guidance, refer back to the color collection of designs following page 16. If you want to indicate color right on your canvas, paint on the pattern with acrylic paints, thinned with water if necessary. The paint is available in tubes or bottles at art supply stores and is water soluble when wet, but impervious to water and cleaning fluids when dry.

*Stitching Technique*

Each stitch is made in the following way:

Fold one piece of yarn over the shank of the latch hook (see Fig. 31). Place the hook into one hole and bring it up under the thread and out of the hole just above (see

Fig. 32); it doesn't matter if the hook points to the right or left.

Catch both ends of the yarn over the latch and under the hook (see Fig. 32a).

Hold the yarn ends with one hand as you draw the hook toward you with the other. The latch will close automatically against the hook and over the yarn; the yarn ends will be drawn through the mesh holes and the looped yarn as you pull the hook toward you, securing the stitch around the canvas thread (see Fig. 32b).

Remove the hook and tug on the yarn ends to tighten the knot (see Fig. 32c). If the ends of yarn aren't even (because you didn't center the piece of yarn on the shank of the hook), pull on the shorter end to create an even pile.

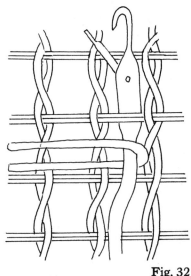

Fig. 32

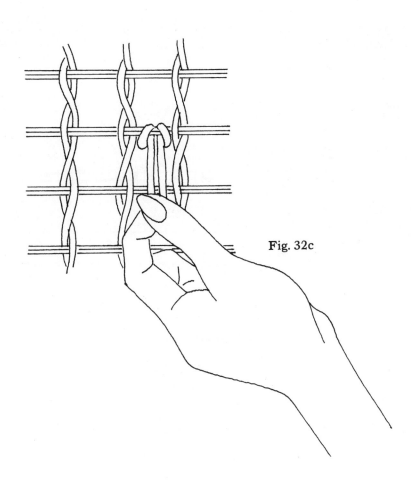

Fig. 32c

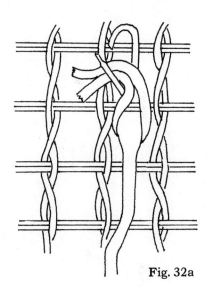

Fig. 32a

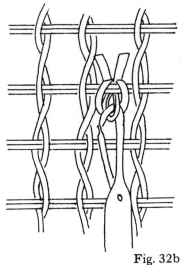

Fig. 32b

## WORKING THE DESIGN

Lay the canvas on your lap with the selvage at your left and work the project from bottom to top. If you are right handed, you may be more comfortable starting at the right edge of the bottom line and working toward the left edge; if you are left handed, you may prefer to start at the left side and work toward the right. You can work in either direction, or even from the center out toward both sides. The important point is to work from bottom to top, so that the tails of the newly formed stitches fall over those below them (see Fig. 33). As you can see, as you work across each row you will be using whatever color yarn the design calls for, rather than completing individual areas of color as a unit.

As you work your design, keep the canvas flat on your lap. When you have stitched too many rows to work comfortably in that position, fold the canvas horizontally along the next row to be stitched (see Fig. 34), tucking the completed work underneath as you fold each successive row to be worked.

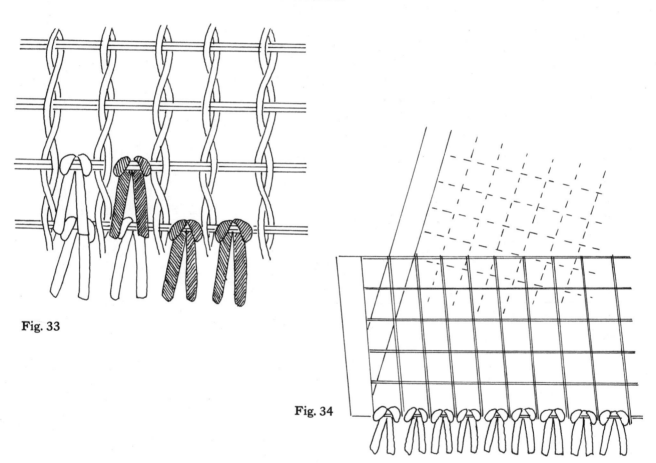

Fig. 33

Fig. 34

### Stitching Hints and Reminders

\*\*\* Always insert your latch hook into the canvas in the same direction, so that all the stitches fall the same way and the tails of each stitch point downward.

\*\*\* Make a stitch in every canvas hole. An unfilled mesh creates a readily apparent gap in the pile surface.

\*\*\* When confronted with a choice of color at the point where you change from one to another, put the project on the floor and choose the color that best completes the design as your eye sees it from a distance.

## FINISHING THE RUG

After you have hooked the design, check the underside to be sure that you have not skipped any of the meshes. If you need to insert additional stitches, push away the tails of stitches lying above so that they will not become entangled in the newly formed loops (see Fig. 35).

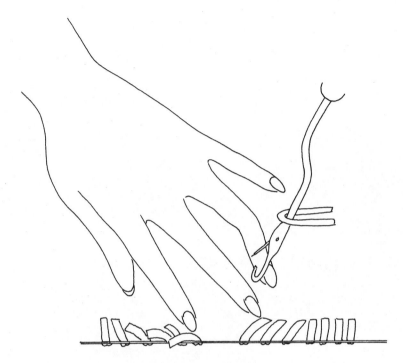

Fig. 35

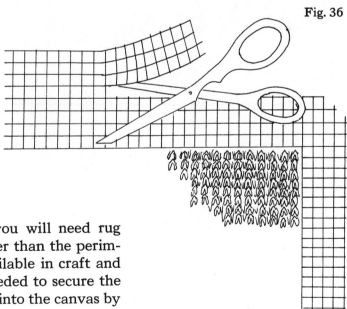

Fig. 36

To finish your rug or hanging you will need rug binding 1½ inches wide and a little longer than the perimeter of the project. Binding is widely available in craft and sewing shops. No protective coating is needed to secure the stitches, as they are already firmly locked into the canvas by the latch hook.

On all sides of the project cut the canvas to within one inch of the stitches. At the corners, cut to within one inch of the corner stitches (see Fig. 36).

Lay the project face up on a table or the floor. Around the outside edges place the binding so it lies primarily over the stitches rather than over the unworked canvas hem (see Fig. 37).

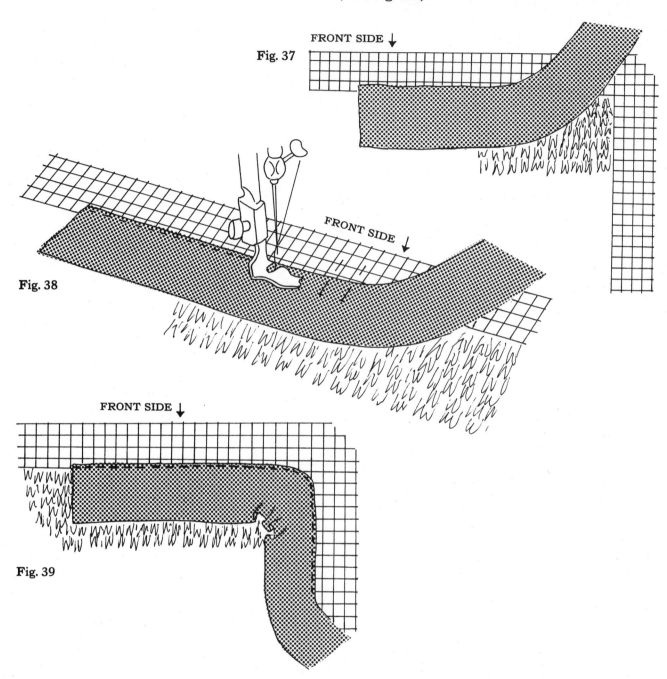

FRONT SIDE ↓

Fig. 37

FRONT SIDE ↓

Fig. 38

FRONT SIDE ↓

Fig. 39

Pin the binding in place, keeping it slack as you attach it. Then sew its outer edge to the canvas hem, as close as possible to the hooked stitches (see Fig. 38). As you turn the corners or a curve, the binding will tend to bunch toward its inner edge (see Fig. 39). This will be corrected shortly.

When you have sewn the rug binding around the perimeter of the project, cut away any excess length (see

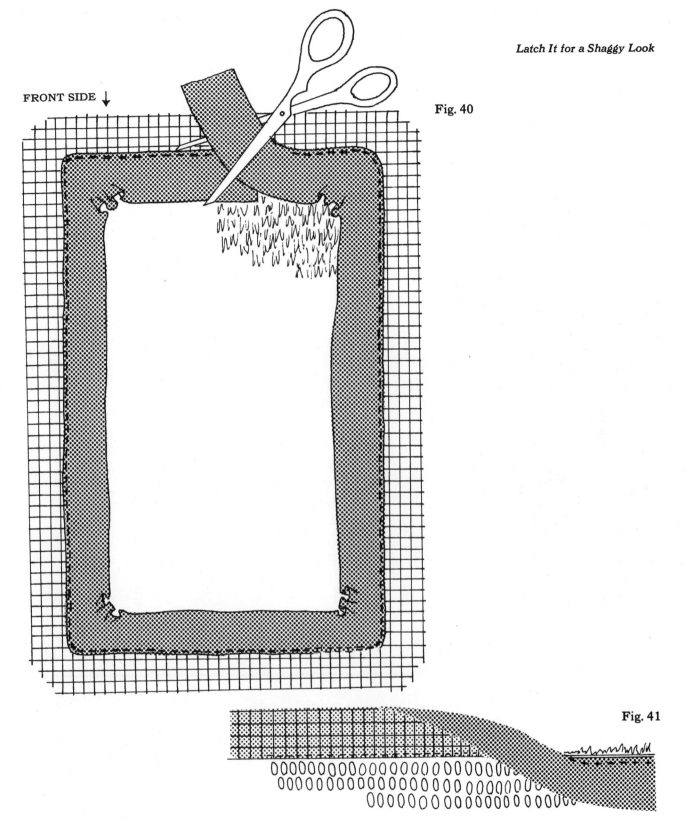

FRONT SIDE ↓

Fig. 40

Fig. 41

Fig. 40). It is not necessary to turn under the cut edges of the binding.

Turn the project face down so the back of the stitching faces you. Reaching under the project, bring the loose edge of the binding around toward you; the unworked canvas hem will come with it (see Fig. 41). Pull the rug binding far enough to the back so that no canvas shows from the side, but not so tightly that the edge of the rug curls up. Stitch the rug binding down through the canvas on all sides (see Fig. 42).

As you come to the corners, tuck the excess rug binding and canvas into a neat fold or miter and tack the folded binding along the mitered corner, if necessary (see Fig. 43). As you work around curves, occasionally take up excess canvas and rug binding into pleats (see Fig. 44).

If you want a more elaborate finish or trim, or a lining, or want to display your rug as a wall hanging, see "Final Touches," page 125, for more ideas.

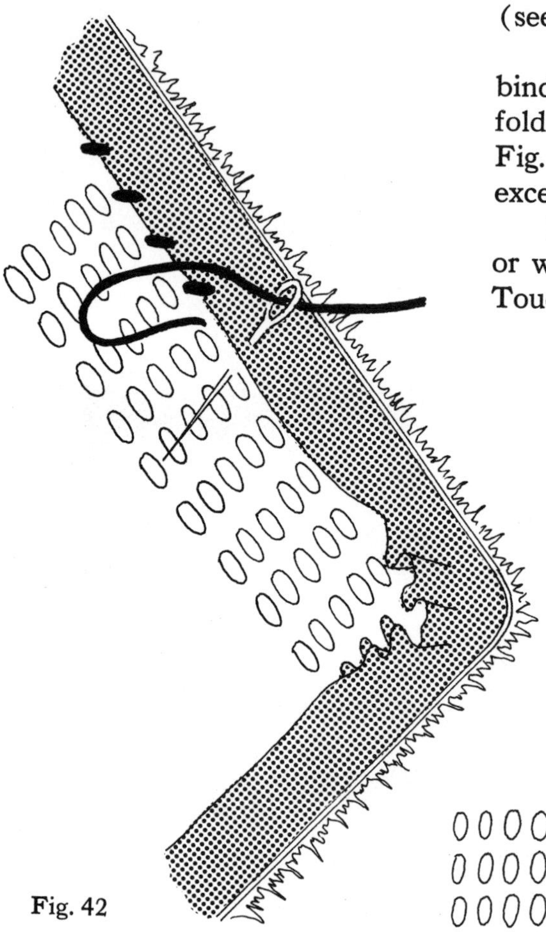

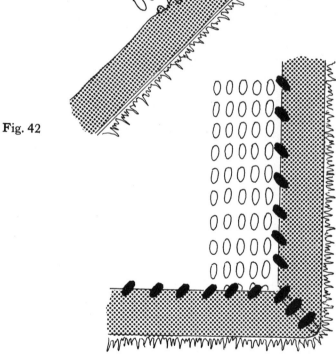

Fig. 42

Fig. 43

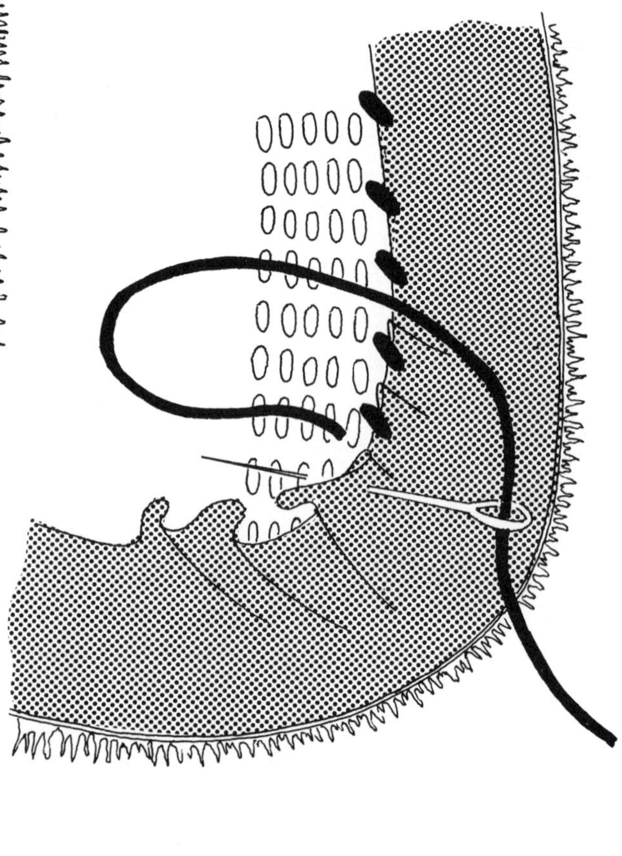

Fig. 44

# Needlepoint It For a Flat Look

CHAPTER

5

## TOOLS OF THE TRADE

To make a needlepoint rug you will need the following equipment:

  canvas
  needle
  yarn
  masking tape

### Canvas

Although needlepoint rugs can be made on canvas of any size mesh, beginners will find No. 5 interlocking canvas the most useful. This canvas, coarsely woven of white cotton, has five holes to the inch (which give the canvas its designation). The mesh is formed by pairs of vertical threads twisted around and interlocking with each pair of closely spaced horizontal threads (see Fig. 46). It is 40 inches wide.

Note: Don't confuse No. 5 interlocking canvas with No. 5 penelope canvas, also a double-thread mesh but more difficult to stitch because the two horizontal and two vertical threads are more widely spaced, creating a confusing grid of small mesh squares for beginners (see Fig. 46a).

With the selvage of the canvas running vertically, cut the canvas two inches larger on all sides than your design. Prepare a rectangular (or square) canvas even if the design is round or irregular in shape. Bind the cut edges with masking tape to prevent raveling (see Fig. 47).

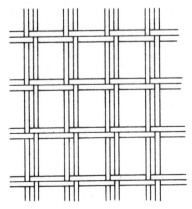

Fig. 45

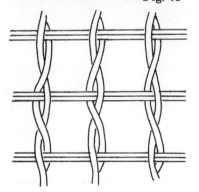

Fig. 46

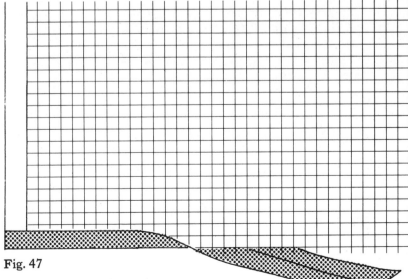

Fig. 47

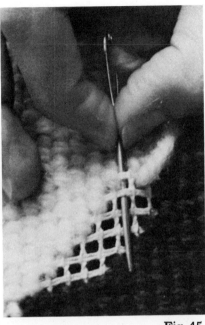

Fig. 46a

87

### Needle

Needles for needlepoint have blunt points and long tapered eyes. Try either No. 13 or No. 14 with No. 5 interlocking canvas. The correct needle for any canvas has a shaft slender enough to pass easily through the mesh and an eye large enough to accommodate the yarn comfortably.

### Yarn

Rug yarn is fairly heavy in weight, and plump and springy enough to cover the mesh in a No. 5 canvas. Offered by a number of manufacturers, it is usually sold by the ounce or the skein, and sometimes you can buy it by the strand or fraction-of-an-ounce. The best quality for rugmaking is pure wool, which has the strength to withstand abrasion and wear; cotton, rayon, synthetics, and blends are available and can be incorporated into wall hangings which don't require durability.

The color range in needlepoint rug yarns is appealingly broad. Paternayan Bros., Inc., for example, offers a breathtaking range of 216 colors grouped in "families" in its Pat-Rug wool. DMC and Nantucket Needleworks each has a more limited though attractive palette.

*Estimating your yarn needs.* The best estimate is the one you make yourself, as follows:

1. Cut and measure a length of the yarn you will be using.

2. With that piece of yarn, work up one square inch (25 stitches) on the No. 5 rug canvas, using the basket-weave stitch (or whatever stitch you plan to use).

3. Measure the amount of yarn left in your needle to ascertain how much of the original length of yarn went into the 25 stitches.

4. Compute the number of square inches in your project. For example, a rug measuring 2 by 4 feet contains 1,152 square inches.

5. Multiply the number of square inches in your rug (Step 4) with the amount of yarn needed for one square inch (Step 3) to compute your total yarn needs.

6. Estimate the area for each color yarn and apportion the yarn total among them.

Note: If you are using Pat-Rug wool, here is a general guide: one strand about 2 yards long covers 2¼ to 3 inches, or about 72 stitches.

*** Buy generous amounts of yarn in the same dye lots, especially for the background or large areas of color where a change in dye lot is particularly noticeable. Unused yarn of one or more ounces can usually be returned.

*Putting the Design on the Backing*

With your life-size design in hand (as described in the chapter on "Enlarging the Designs"), you are ready to transfer it to your prepared rug canvas.

1. Be sure the enlarged design is outlined in bold dark lines. If any of the lines are fuzzy or indistinct, go over them with a black waterproof marker.

2. Lay the enlarged design face up, and over it position the rug canvas with the selvage running up and down. Tape the design and canvas together. The darkened lines of the design should be clearly visible through the mesh of the rug canvas, but if you want even more visibility, work on a white table top or on the floor over a white sheet.

3. Trace the design onto the rug canvas with a waterproof marker (see Fig. 48). This marker need not be black; in fact, it should not be dark in areas of light color, but it must be waterproof.

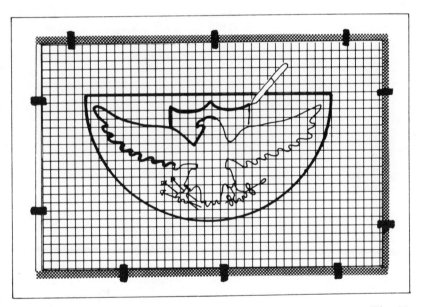

Fig. 48

4. For color guidance, refer back to the color collection of designs following page 16. If you want to indicate color right on your canvas, paint the pattern with acrylic paints, thinned with water if necessary. The paint is available in tubes or bottles at art supply stores and is water soluble when wet but impervious to water and cleaning fluids when dry.

5. Before stitching, outline the entire piece of canvas, including the taped edges—not just the rug design you

will stitch—on a large piece of heavy brown paper (see Fig. 49). This will later be your blocking guide; put it away until ready to block the stitched rug.

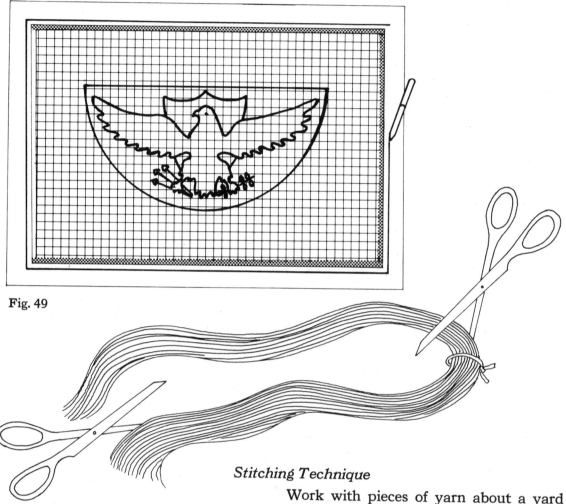

Fig. 49

Fig. 50

### Stitching Technique

Work with pieces of yarn about a yard in length. Longer pieces will tend to fray from being pulled through the canvas mesh too many times; shorter lengths will waste too much wool in starting and ending. With the highly recommended Pat-Rug wool which comes in skeins, a good working length is obtained by cutting the skein twice—once at each end (see Fig. 50). This is the way needlework shops cut their yarn when they sell less than a skein.

Now thread your needle, folding one end of the length of yarn over the pointed end of the needle and then pinching the fold together as you withdraw the needle (see Fig. 51). Insert the doubled fold through the eye of the needle and pull the yarn through.

Of the three basic needlepoint stitches—basket-weave, continental, half cross—only basketweave offers all the qualities required in a needlepoint rug: a tightly woven stitch that covers the canvas well, provides a nicely padded backing on the underside, and only distorts the canvas to a minimal degree. This last consideration is the most impor-

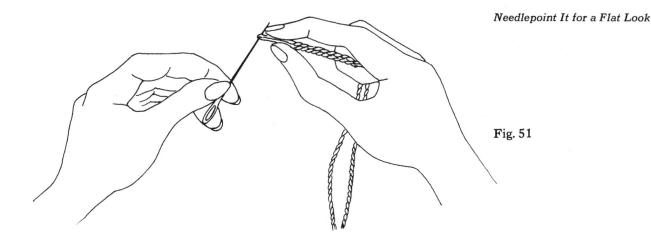

Fig. 51

tant, because the neat appearance of a properly aligned rug rests primarily with even-handed stitching; there is no frame or mounting to keep the rug aligned, and blocking will only correct moderate distortion. For these reasons, the basic stitch recommended for needlepoint rugmaking is the basketweave.

The basketweave stitch is actually a succession of identical stitches, each of which crosses the intersections of the canvas from one mesh at the southwest corner to the opposite mesh in the northeast corner (see Fig. 52). The sequence of the stitches—that is, the order in which they are laid on the canvas—is important. As you can see in Fig. 53, the stitches are worked in diagonal rows, starting at the top right corner of the canvas (or of any design area within it), if you are right handed. In alternating directions, it moves first up the canvas from right to left, then down the canvas from left to right. The same sequence of stitches is maintained no matter what shape area you are covering (see Fig. 54).

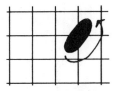

Fig. 52

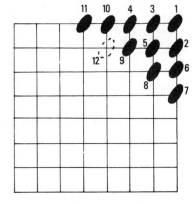

Fig. 53

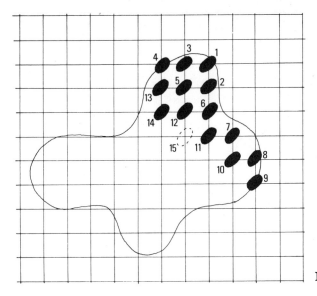

Fig. 54

The actual "fingering" of the basketweave stitch is given in Figs. 55 and 56. Bring the needle up through the canvas from the back to the front at *1* and at every subsequent odd number; push it down through the canvas from front to back at *2* and at every subsequent even number. As soon as you do a few stitches, you will see that the stitching pattern has a logical rhythm that is easy to follow.

Note: If you are left handed, start at the bottom left corner. Fingering for left-handed stitchers is the mirror image (see Fig. 57), as is the sequence of stitches (see Fig. 58).

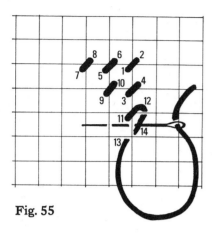

**Fig. 55**

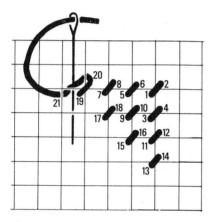

**Fig. 56**

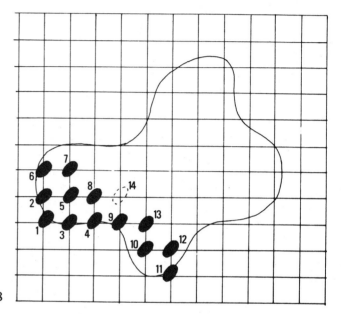

**Fig. 58**

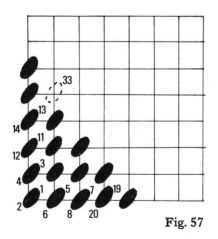

**Fig. 57**

When you start to stitch, leave an inch or two of yarn at the back as you come up through the canvas for your first stitch (see Fig. 59). Hold this tail of yarn with your free hand while you complete a few more stitches which will cover and anchor the yarn end (see Fig. 60). Follow this same procedure as you start each new length of yarn.

When you have worked the yarn to within two inches of its end, finish it off by slipping it through the backs of the last few stitches you have made. Clip the tag ends of all finished threads as you go, so they don't become entangled in your working thread.

## WORKING THE DESIGN

Stitch the design elements first, whether they are central motifs or allover patterns, and leave the background to last. If you have a choice, work darker-colored areas of the design before the lighter-colored areas to minimize soiling.

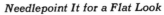

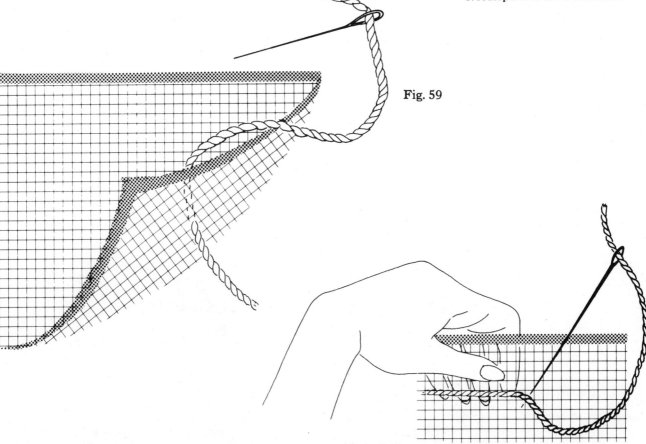

Fig. 59

Fig. 60

When you come to odd shapes in which you cannot maintain the basketweave pattern precisely, you can interrupt the diagonal sequence and insert or skip individual stitches wherever necessary to complete the design. In Fig. 61 you can see where individual stitches have been added and in Fig. 62 where they have been omitted.

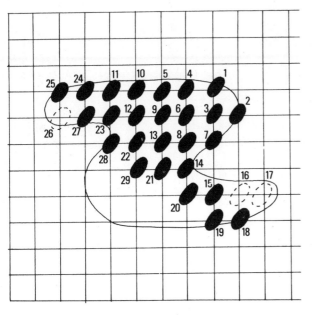

Fig. 61

Fig. 62

Fig. 63

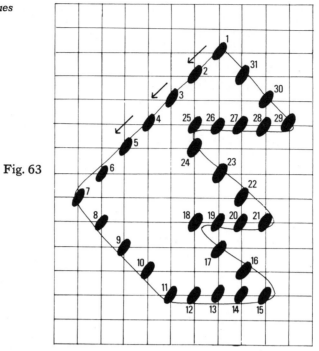

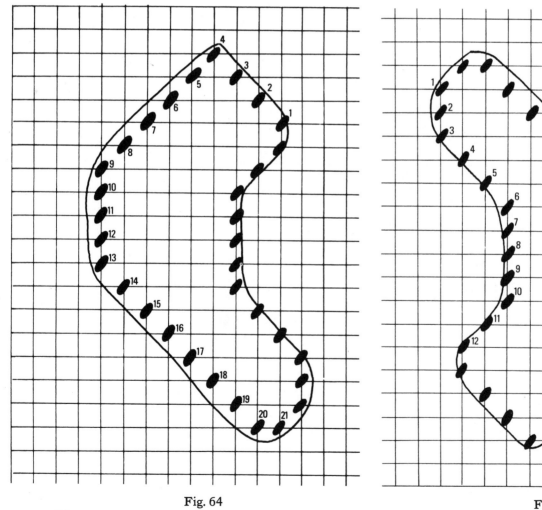

Fig. 64

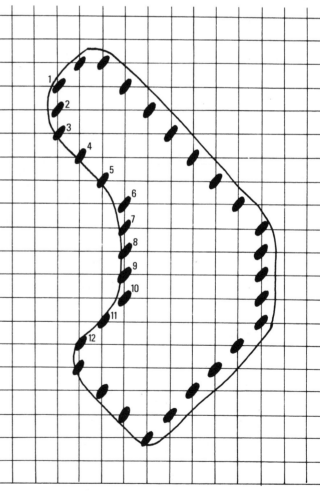

Fig. 65

If you are faced with a complicated motif that cannot be completed easily with the insertion of a few individual stitches here and there, first outline the entire shape and then fill it in. To do this, make a series of stitches—horizontally, vertically, diagonally, left or right—that follow the outline of the motif (see Fig. 63). The only direction in which you cannot stitch is to the "northeast," so when you want to outline an area to the right and above where you are working, simply turn the entire canvas upside down, and you will see that your area is now to the left and below where you can easily continue your outlining (see Figs. 64 and 65).

When you have outlined the design element, fill it in with stitches made in the regular basketweave sequence (see Fig. 66).

When you have completed stitching all the design motifs, start the background in the upper right corner of

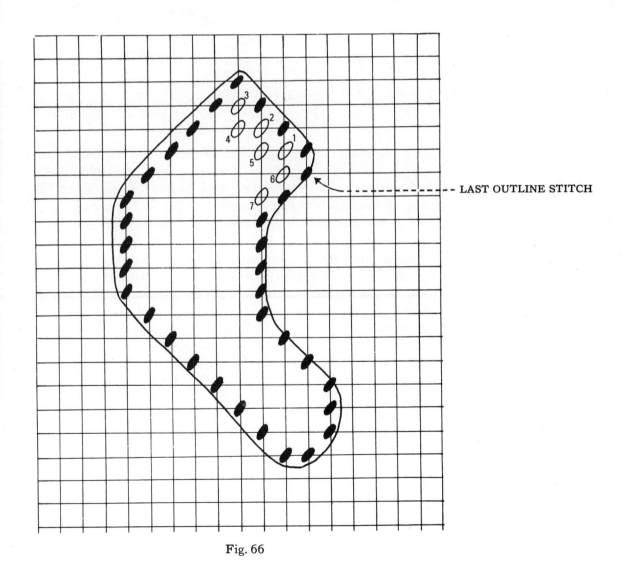

LAST OUTLINE STITCH

Fig. 66

the canvas (the lower left corner if you are left handed). Stitch the background rows in basketweave sequence, from one edge of the rug to another (see Fig. 67). When your background rows are interrupted by an area of already-stitched design, work back and forth on one side of the design until your background rows can clear the design and continue on the other side of it (see Fig. 68). Don't work back and forth across the design, or you'll create excessive padding on the back.

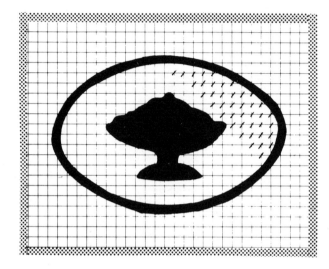

Fig. 67

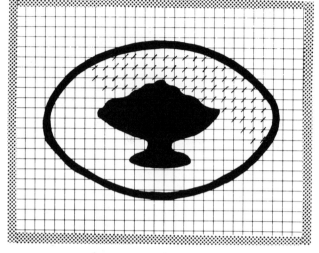

Fig. 68

Note: It is important to continue your background rows across the canvas whenever that is possible—that is, when there is no intervening design—because each row linking two separate areas provides a guide for maintaining the overall basketweave sequence of alternating up/down rows. You may sometimes find yourself with lone "fingers" of background rows penetrating otherwise unstitched background areas. Simply fill those areas in, taking care to resume stitching in the correct up or down row; you will see that eventually all background areas will meet in proper alternating sequence. In Fig. 69 the arrows indicate the correct starting points for various stitching areas so the correct alternating order is maintained.

*Stitching Hints and Reminders*

\*\*\* Work every row with an even hand, exerting the same amount of tension or pull on threads as you go up and down the canvas. An uneven tug on the threads from one direction is what causes distortion of the canvas and pulls it from a rectangle to a parallelogram.

\*\*\* Make your stitches with fairly slack yarn so they are loose and plump enough to cover the canvas nicely. Don't worry about working too loosely; in the unlikely event that your stitches really are too loose, you can tighten them

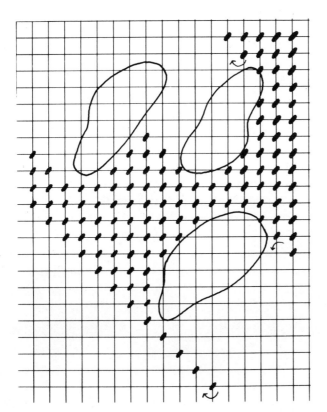

Fig. 69

easily from the underside later. But if they are even slightly tight, they may leave bare canvas showing and pull the work out of shape.

   \*\*\* For the best canvas coverage try to keep your yarn flat and untwisted as you work. The yarn has a tendency to become more tightly twisted by the stitching motion of your hand, and you can correct this by occasionally holding the canvas upside down and letting the threaded needle unwind by itself (see Fig. 70).

Fig. 70

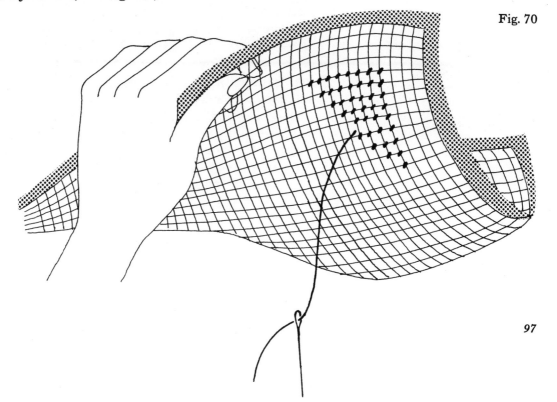

\*\*\* Be careful to alternate the up and down rows as you work. If you stitch two contiguous rows in the same direction, a slight ridge will form where the interlocking basketweave pattern has been interrupted. To avoid this, get in the habit of stopping work in the middle of a row, putting it away with the needle set in the next mesh to be worked (see Fig. 71).

\*\*\* One of the seeming puzzles of needlepoint is how to express a curved line on the horizontal-vertical grid of the canvas. As you work these curved lines, traced from the design enlargement, simply make your stitches on the canvas intersections that are closest to the drawn line (see Fig. 72). You can see that sometimes your stitch will be on one side of the line, sometimes on the other, and once in a while it may even be right on the line. But even though a "curved" line will be a series of steps on close inspection, from a distance it will appear curved because your eye will round them off.

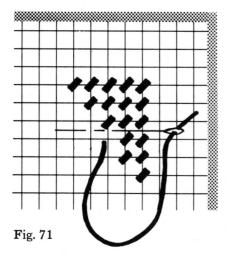

Fig. 71

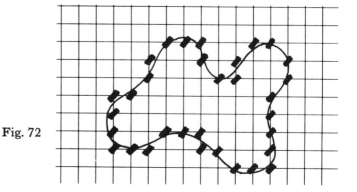

Fig. 72

\*\*\* When you have finished stitching one area of color, finish off the yarn end and cut it before moving on to another area of the same color. Don't carry the threaded needle over the intervening canvas or weave it through an interlying patch of stitching.

\*\*\* Rug-size projects are often bulky to handle, particularly if you are stitching an interior section of the canvas. You may find it helpful to roll up the canvas on either side of the area in which you are working (see Fig. 73). Anchor the rolls through the canvas mesh with large safety pins or with extra tapestry needles, taking care not to split the canvas threads.

\*\*\* If you want to remove one or more just-completed stitches, unthread your needle, pick the stitches loose with the point, and pull the yarn out carefully. Don't poke the threaded needle back through the canvas in the hope of retracing the stitch and thus removing it; you will almost certainly split the yarn in the back with your needle and compound the difficulty.

\*\*\* After you have stitched the design, check the entire project carefully to be sure you haven't missed any

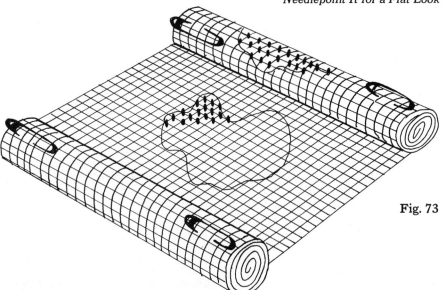

Fig. 73

of the intersections. Missed stitches are sometimes hard to catch, especially if the design has been painted on the canvas in lifelike colors. Sometimes you can find the bare spots by holding the canvas up to the light, but don't substitute this light test for a close scrutiny of the needlepoint. Naturally, fill in missing stitches with the appropriate color yarn.

    \*\*\* If patches of bare canvas show through, not because stitches are missing but because they were pulled too tight to cover the threads properly or because the rug yarn wore thin, go over these skimpy stitches with one or two plies of your rug yarn. You can easily separate your yarn into its component plies by pulling them apart (see Fig. 74).

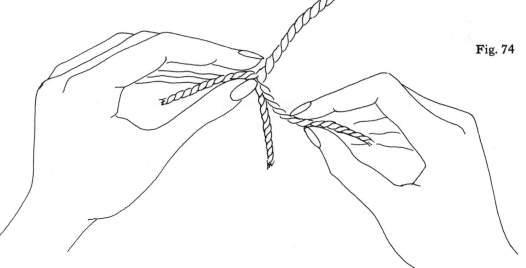

Fig. 74

## BLOCKING THE RUG

    All needlepoint rugs should be blocked for two reasons: First, to correct the distortion that inevitably creeps into the rug, no matter how carefully you work. Second, to give a neat finish to the stitches, smoothing out any bumps or irregularities on the surface.

After you have checked your rug thoroughly, block it according to these instructions:

1. Take the brown paper blocking guide you have put aside (see page 90) and tack it to a piece of board or plywood that is at least as large as the canvas you have been working. You might have to use an old door or even the wooden floor of an attic.

2. Lay the needlepoint face down on the brown paper. Match the upper right and the upper left corners of the needlepoint stitching with the two upper corners of the outline on the brown paper, then tack each corner through the taped edge with rustproof pins or tacks (see Fig. 75). You can see how much the canvas has been pulled out of shape by how far it is out of "sync" with the outline on the brown paper.

3. When the two upper corners have been firmly secured, lay a wet towel over the back of the project until the stitches become damp and pliant but not soaking. You will find that now it will be easier to pull the canvas into shape, making it conform to the outline on the brown paper.

4. When the entire rug is flexible and pliant, pull the bottom two corners into shape and tack them so that

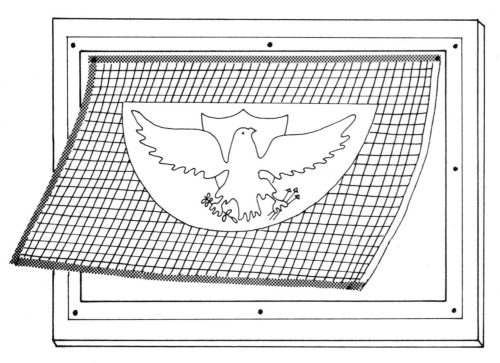

Fig. 75

Fig. 76

the corners of the needlepoint stitching match the corners of the outline, as in Step 3. You will find that you probably cannot pull the rug into conformity with the outline in one movement; you'll have to pull and tug a bit at a time, working from side to side and tacking and retacking along the sides until the bottom half matches the blocking outline (see Fig. 76). You may have to redampen the back of the stitching periodically to keep it flexible.

5. When all four corners are aligned properly, tack all the sides at one-inch intervals. Your tacks will hold most securely through the taped edges, but you can also tack through the canvas mesh—not through the canvas threads—if you want to correct some special distortions (see Fig. 77).

6. With the canvas tacked firmly in place, dampen the back of the rug once more.

7. Leave the tacked rug on the blocking board in a horizontal position until it is completely dry; this will take a few days. Keep it out of direct sunlight.

Note: A severely distorted rug may have to be blocked more than once.

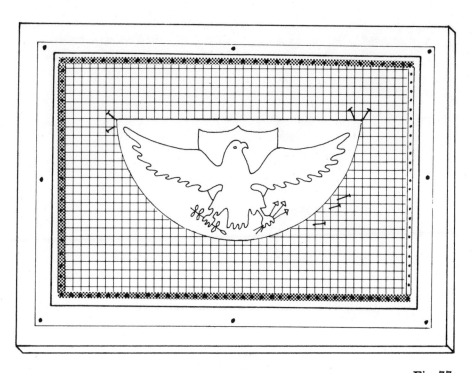

Fig. 77

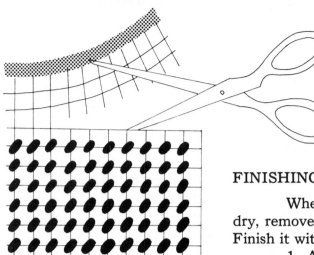

Fig. 78

## FINISHING THE RUG

When the rug has been blocked and is thoroughly dry, remove it from the blocking board and brown paper. Finish it with an overcasting stitch as follows:

1. Along all sides cut the excess unworked canvas border to within one row of the stitched needlepoint (see Fig. 78). You can see that one unstitched thread of canvas is visible around all sides.

2. Along these cut edges make a row of overcasting stitches which includes both the outer unstitched thread of canvas and the outermost row of needlepoint stitches (see Fig. 79). As you turn the corners, you will have to make three or even four overcasting stitches in the corner mesh in order to get sufficient yarn coverage (see Fig. 80).

If your rug has shaped, curved or diagonal edges, cut the excess unworked canvas border the equivalent of one row outside the existing needlepoint stitching, always leaving at least one unworked canvas thread to protect the needlepoint (see Fig. 81). Work the overcasting row as de-

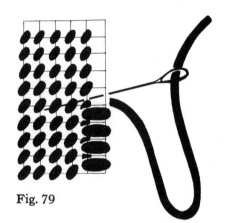

Fig. 79

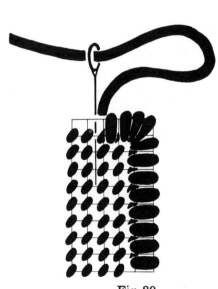

Fig. 80

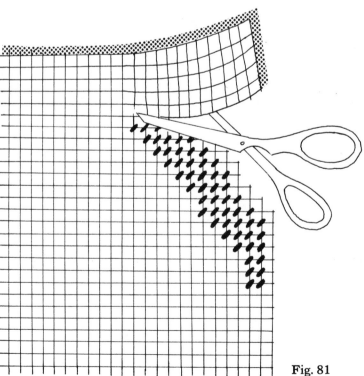

Fig. 81

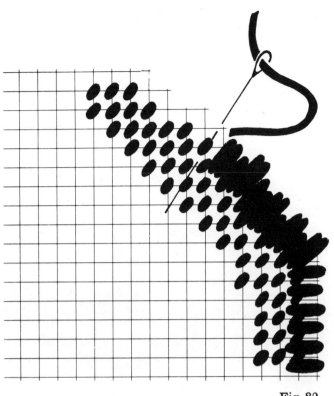

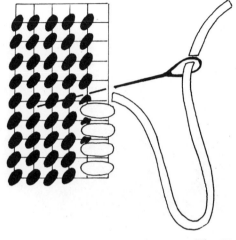

Fig. 82

Fig. 83

scribed above, always covering both the outermost row of needlepoint stitches and one row of unstitched canvas thread, even if it isn't the same unstitched canvas thread. Make extra overcasting stitches around the curves as needed for full coverage (see Fig. 82).

\*\*\* If you find that the rug yarn you have been using doesn't give full enough coverage in the overcasting stitch, add one or two extra plies of the same yarn to your needle.

\*\*\* If you want to create a narrow border around your rug, make the overcasting stitches in a contrasting color yarn (see Fig. 83).

\*\*\* If you want the most inconspicuous edging, work the overcasting stitches in the color or colors that appear in the outermost row of needlepoint (see Fig. 84). If there is a multi-color design at the edge, you may want to work with several needles threaded with each color yarn, changing needles to match the changing design. Carry the idle threads under the overcast edge as you work (see Fig. 84).

If you want a more elaborate finish or trim, or a lining, or want to display your rug as a wall hanging, see "Final Touches," page 125, for more ideas.

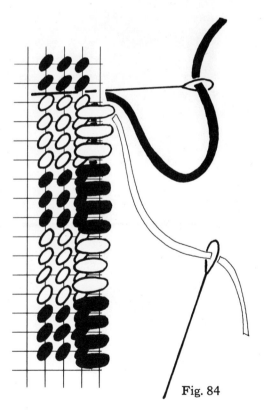

Fig. 84

CHAPTER

# 6

# *Punch It
For a Loopy Look*

## TOOLS OF THE TRADE

To make a punch-hooked rug or wall hanging, you will need the following equipment:

backing fabric
a punch hook
yarn
wooden frame

Fig. 85

Fig. 86

### *Backing Fabric*

Almost any kind of woven material can be used as a backing fabric as long as the weave is tight enough to grip the yarn loops. In practice, this is usually cotton or linen fabric woven with about 12 to 15 horizontal and vertical threads to each square inch. Use more tightly woven backings for thinner yarns, looser weaves for thicker yarns, looking for the happy choice that will hold the yarn securely yet not tire your hand as you push the punch hook through it.

Cotton and linen are the most durable of backing fabrics, and are especially recommended for rug wear. They are sold by the yard in various widths ranging up to 15 feet under such names as Duraback, monk's cloth, cotton warp cloth, cotton hopsacking.

Wall hangings, which don't receive the same abrasive wear as rugs, can be punched on less sturdy materials like burlap. Although the jute threads of burlap tend to break under wear, making burlap unsuitable underfoot,

*104*

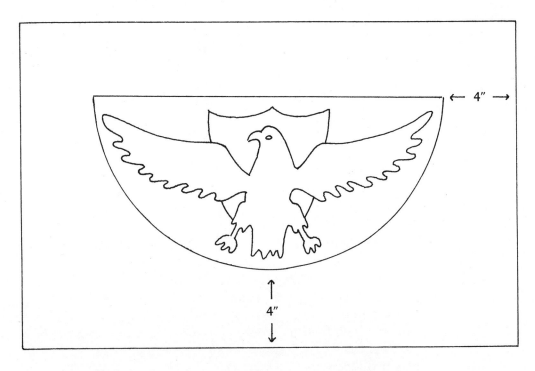

Fig. 87

they have an interesting texture which can be incorporated into a wall hanging by leaving portions of the backing unstitched. A similar decorative element can be achieved by using a patterned or printed backing on which areas are left unstitched; you can see this technique in the photograph of the doll hanging, opposite.

Whichever fabric you choose for your backing, cut it 4 inches larger on all sides than your design. You will need this allowance for tacking to your frame and for the outermost stitches to clear the frame itself. No matter what the shape of your design, cut the backing material in a rectangle (or square), measuring the 4-inch allowance from the widest points of the design (see Fig. 87).

If your backing material tends to ravel easily, turn the cut edges under the hem (see Fig. 88). Otherwise, no special preparation is needed. Slight fraying is not a problem, as long as the hem allowance is the full 4 inches.

Fig. 88

## Punch Hooks

There are different kinds of speed hooks, but they all perform the same function—pushing the yarn through the backing fabric to create loops.

The shuttle hook (Fig. 89) uses a double-handed motion to operate the two parts of the hook—the needle and the foot—that alternately slide back and forth. The needle pushes the yarn loop through the backing; the foot holds it in place while the needle "walks" forward to form the next loop.

Another type of punch hook comes with two different needles—one for light-weight knitting worsteds, the other for heavier-weight rug yarns. Each needle can be adjusted to form loops of varying heights, ranging from ¼ inch to ¾ inch high (see Fig. 89a).

The simplest punch needle is a pointed tube embedded in a handle (see Fig. 89b). It is satisfactory for all-purpose rugmaking when you use rug yarn and it forms loops about ½ inch high. Some types include a gauge which can produce even shorter loops.

Instructions for threading the needles are supplied with the tool itself. Except for differences in assembling and threading, the following information applies to all punch hooks.

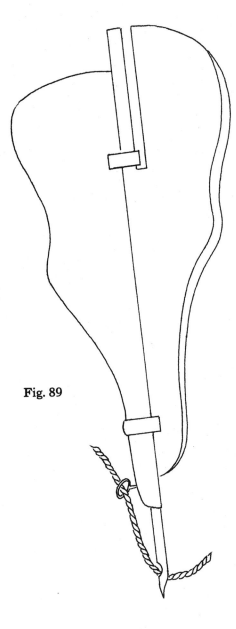

Fig. 89

## Yarn

Any kind of material can be used in a punch hook as long as it passes through the eye of the needle easily. If it doesn't move through the needle smoothly, it will pull on the stitches, making them uneven or pulling them out of the backing altogether. Most punch hooks are designed for use with rug-weight yarns. A narrow punch needle can accommodate light-weight yarn, and a standard punch needle can hold two or even three strands of worsted. The only requirement is that the yarn travel freely through the needle without slipping out of the channel. A yarn that is too fine for the needle will not be securely gripped by the backing because the needle will have punched an oversize hole.

Most popular rug yarns are wool and acrylic, both durable and washable. Interesting visual effects are possible with cotton yarns, linen, nylon, leather strips, plastic, felt —in fact, any kind of fabric that can be cut into strips thin enough to pass through the eye of the punch needle.

Choose your hooking material for its durability, its look and texture, and the eventual use of the finished project. Heavy yarns, for instance, are more durable in high-pile work than are light yarns, and obviously they cover the field with fewer stitches. Light worsteds can lend precision and grace to a design outline, but may not cover the background as satisfactorily as heavy yarn.

All materials tend to behave a little differently when actually stitched, so try out different yarns before making a final choice. You will find that some yarn loops spread out and cover the backing well while others twist tightly together and require less space between stitches.

For this reason, yarn estimates are rarely reliable since they depend on so many variable factors: the height of the loops, the spacing between the loops and between rows, and the weight of the yarn. The needlework shop where you buy your supplies will help you estimate amounts. Buy generous quantities of each dye lot; you can usually return unopened skeins of yarn.

Note: Try to buy your yarns in pull skeins. If not available, wind the yarn into a free-pulling ball before threading your needle.

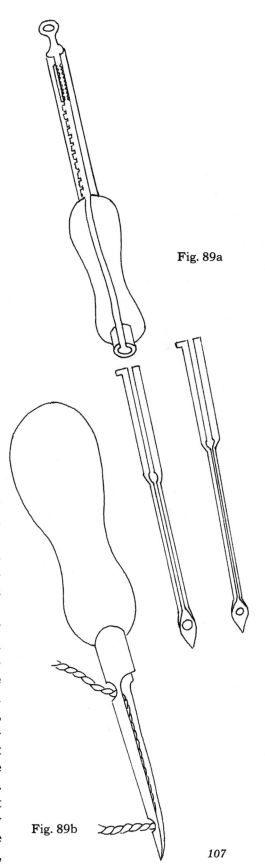

Fig. 89a

Fig. 89b

*Frame*

The backing fabric must be stretched taut across a frame to provide the surface tension necessary for proper punch hooking. There are many types of frames for this purpose, some fairly elaborate, with tilt tops and adjustable height stands, that are available from needlework shops or department stores. But the simplest kinds, utilizing discarded picture frames or artist's stretchers, work just as well.

The frame need not encompass the entire rug or hanging at the same time; a frame smaller than your design can be moved around on the backing to accommodate different areas to be stitched. It is more important that the frame be comfortable to work with; if it is too large, you will have trouble reaching the center portions, and if too small, you will have to retack the backing too often. A frame measuring about 24 by 30 inches is a good all-purpose size, but consider any dimensions between 18 and 30 inches square that suits your reach and the dimensions of your project.

If you want to assemble your own frame, the easiest way to do it is to use artist's stretchers. These are sold by the pair in art supply shops and are available in a wide variety of lengths; between 18 and 30 inches, for example, they are made in inch increments. Their tongue-and-groove construction is designed to match another pair of stretchers, the two pairs easily assembling into a frame without additional fasteners (see Fig. 90).

If you want to construct a heavier-duty frame, use two pairs of 2 x 3's of clear pine or any other wood that resists warping and is soft enough to receive tacks, push pins or staples fairly easily. Reinforce the corners of the frame with angle irons (see Fig. 91).

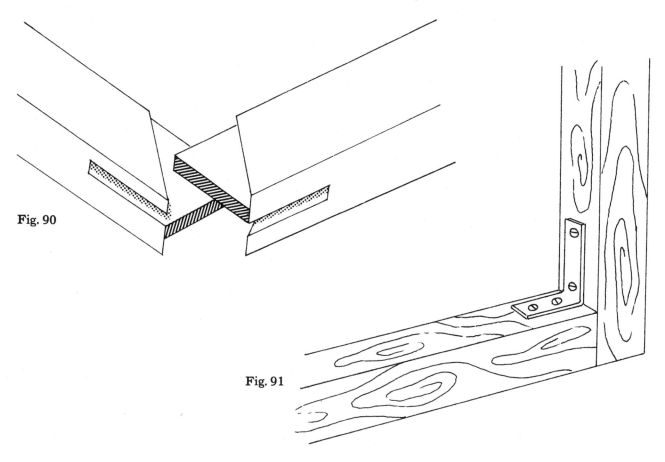

Fig. 90

Fig. 91

## GETTING READY TO WORK

*Putting the Design on the Backing*

With your life-size design in hand (as described in "Enlarging the Designs," page 57), you are ready to transfer it to the backing fabric. You have a choice of ways in which to do this, each offering certain advantages.

1. Hot iron transfer method. Use this if you want your design outlined in thin, sharply defined lines on the backing fabric, if your life-size pattern is drawn on fairly thin paper, and if your design can be punched in reverse. If your design incorporates letters, symbols, or anything else that should not be stitched in its mirror image (which is what happens in the punching process), it is simpler to use one of the following methods.

2. Perforating the pattern. Choose this method if you want your finished project to look just like the design (that is, not a mirror image), and if your life-size pattern is on heavy paper. Perforations tend to tear thin paper, making the pattern difficult to use even once and impossible to re-use.

3. Tracing on a gauze-like fabric. Opt for this method if you want your finished project to look just like the design (not a mirror image), and if your life-size pattern is on tissue, tracing or other thin paper.

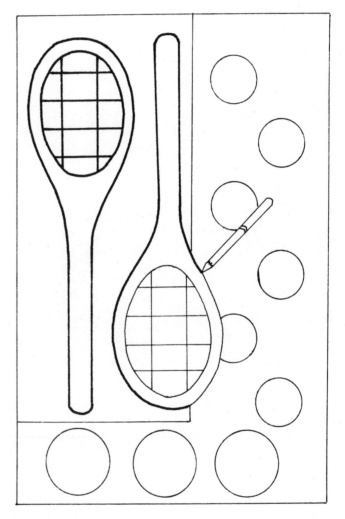

Fig. 92

1. *The hot iron transfer method* requires a special copying pencil available from many needlework and craft shops and by mail order (see "Where to Get What You Need," page 134). Using a sharp point, outline the entire design on your paper pattern with fine firm strokes (see Fig. 92). If you make any mistakes in your outlining, remove them from the paper with an ink eraser or cut them out of the pattern before transferring the design because the dye is difficult to remove from the fabric backing once the design has been transferred.

*109*

Lay the backing material face down and over it position the paper pattern with the outlined design also facing down. Pin or tape the pattern to the backing material to keep it from slipping. Then press the back of the paper pattern with a hot iron to transfer the dye from the outlined design onto the backing material (see Fig. 93). Move the iron slowly over the back of the pattern, covering the surface several times if necessary. Keep the iron as hot as possible without scorching the paper. The dye in the copying pencil works slowly; the thicker the paper you are using, the longer the process will take. Periodically lift one corner of the pattern to check your results.

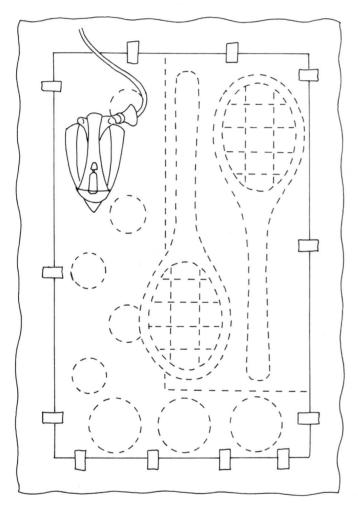

Fig. 93

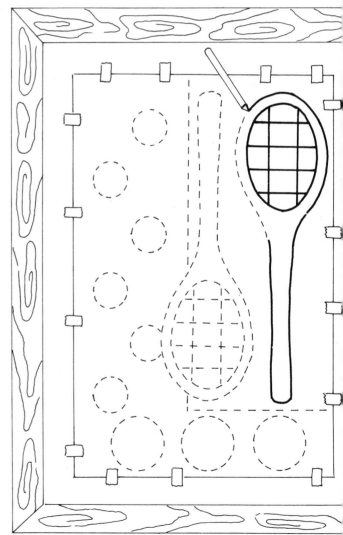

Fig. 94

As you can see, the design that has been transferred to the backing material is the reverse of the way it looks in the design drawing. However, when it has been stitched, it will look just like the original design. If you want your rug to be the mirror image, you must reverse the design itself before transferring. To do this, hold the paper pattern up to the window or another source of light and trace the design with the copying pencil on the *back* of the paper pattern (see Fig. 94). Lay the *traced side* of the paper face down over the backing material and iron over what was originally the top of the life-size pattern (see Fig. 95). Just remember when ironing to make sure that the traced lines made by the special copying pencil are in contact with the backing material.

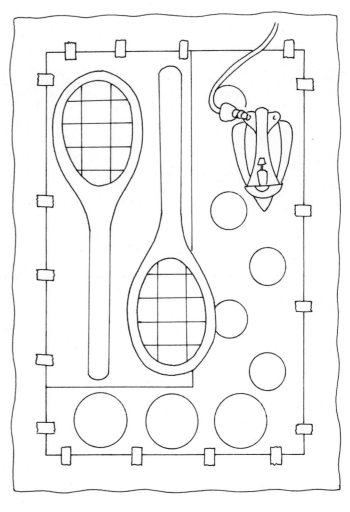

Fig. 95

2. *Perforating the pattern* is an easier way to reverse the design. Using a dressmaker's tracing wheel or a straight pin, make a series of pinholes on all the design lines of your paper pattern (see Fig. 96). Make the holes as close together as you can without tearing the paper pattern.

Note: If you do not want a mirror image of the design, flip the perforated pattern over before transferring it (see Fig. 97).

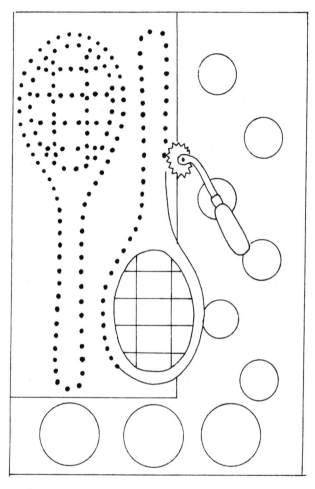

Fig. 96

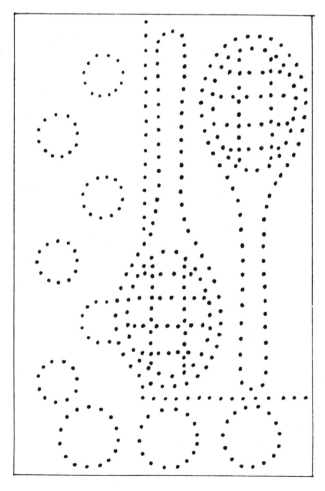

Fig. 97

Lay the backing material face down and over it position the perforated pattern. Pin or tape them together. Ink over the perforated holes very well with the blunt point of an indelible waterproof marking pen to transfer the design to the backing material (see Fig. 98). The closer the perforations, the more solid the design lines on the backing material will appear.

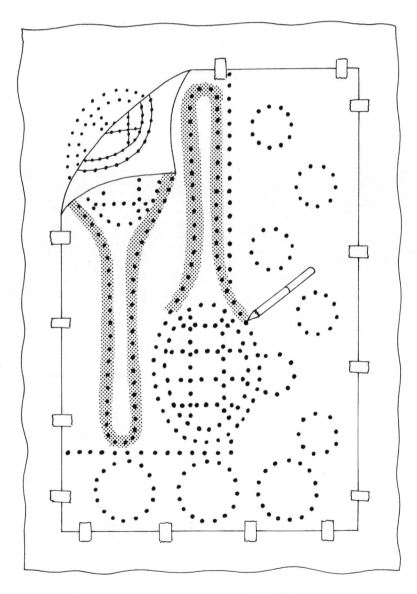

Fig. 98

3. *A gauze tracing* requires a piece of thin, loosely woven fabric like gauze or fine netting slightly larger than your design. Lay the gauzy fabric over the paper pattern and tape it in place. Using an indelible waterproof marking pen trace the lines of the design, which will be clearly visible, onto the gauze fabric (see Fig. 99).

Note: If you do not want a mirror image of the design, turn over the gauze before transferring the design to the backing; you will find that the traced design will show on both sides of the gauze.

Lay the backing material face up and over it position the gauze pattern. Pin or tape them together. With an indelible waterproof marking pen go over the design just outlined on the gauze, thus transferring it to the backing (see Fig. 100). You will find that the more coarsely woven the gauze, the more solid will be the guideline transferred to the backing; more finely woven netting yields a line of individual dots.

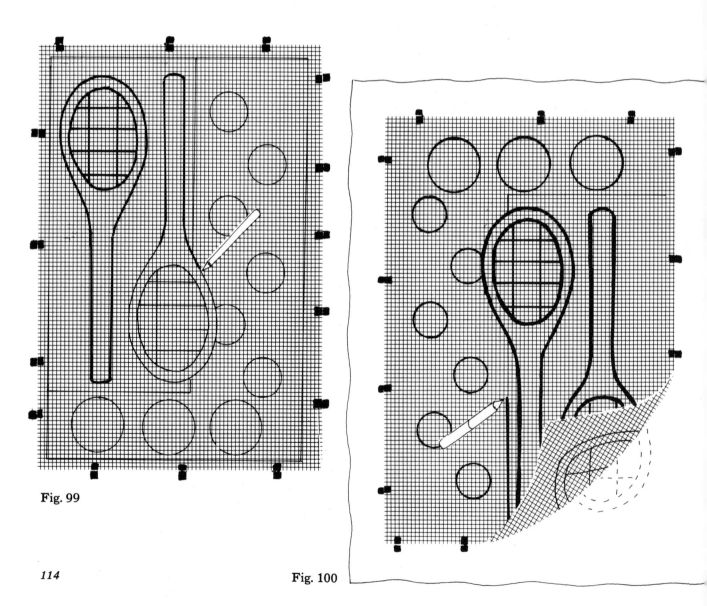

Fig. 99

Fig. 100

For color guidance, refer back to the color collection of designs following page 16. If you want to indicate color right on your backing, paint the pattern with acrylic paints, thinned with water if necessary. The paint is available in tubes or bottles at art supply stores and is water soluble when wet but impervious to water and cleaning fluids when dry.

*Mounting the Backing on the Frame*

Lay the rug backing over the frame with the design facing up. Using tacks, push pins, or a staple gun, first secure the middle of each frame side, then work out towards the corners, alternating sides and pulling the backing material taut as you tack it (see Fig. 101). Keep the backing fabric straight as you secure it; if you tack it even slightly on the bias, you will introduce some slack that will impede the punching motion. Even the most tightly tacked backing tends to loosen from the pressure of punching or from the weight of the yarn, so you may have to retack the backing periodically during the stitching process.

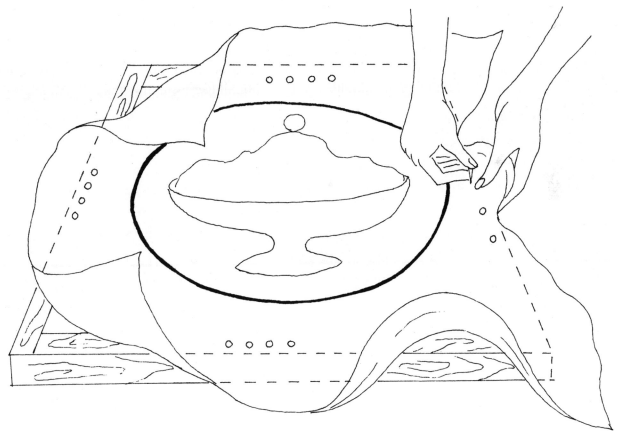

Fig. 101

The backing area to be punched should lie within the open area of the frame. If your frame is larger than your design, or your design is a different shape, you will attach the frame to the 4-inch-wide hem that surrounds the design (see Fig. 101). However, if your frame is smaller than your design, you will have to move the backing around on the frame when you want to stitch different areas. When re-tacking through an already-stitched area, be careful to insert the tacks between, not through, the formed loops (see Fig. 102).

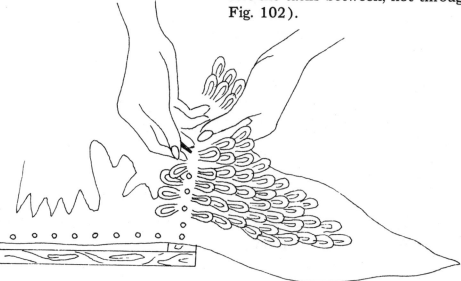

Fig. 102

As you can see, the punch hook requires a clearance of three or four inches beneath the frame to complete the punching motion. Unless you are working on a standing frame, you will have to prop the frame against the edge of a table (see Fig. 103), or over arm rests, or even over two saw horses in the case of a large frame.

Fig. 103

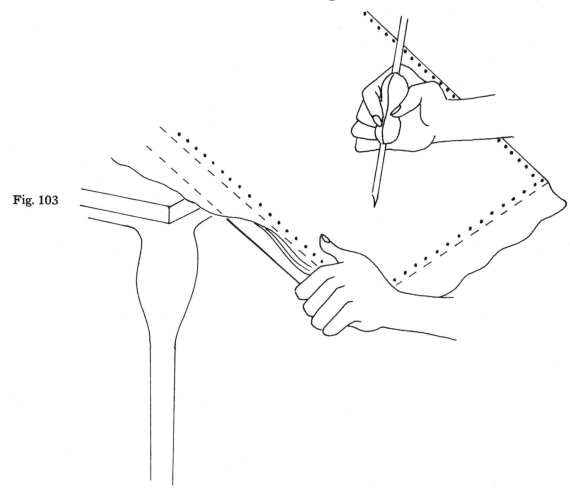

Thread the punch hook according to the instructions which accompany it, and leave a one- or two-inch tail of yarn. Unwind a few feet of yarn. Hold the punch hook with its open channel facing the direction you will be working. Rest your hand on the backing, then plunge the punch hook vertically through the backing up to the handle (see Fig. 104). Keep your hand on the backing while you pull the hook out. Just as it clears the top of the backing, slide the hook forward and plunge it into the backing for the next stitch (see Fig. 105). It is important not to raise the punch hook above the surface lest you pull up the just-formed loop; resting the heel of your hand on the backing helps keep the punch hook gliding along the surface of the backing, thus insuring loops of uniform height. As you can see, you push the hook in from the back, on which the design is outlined, to form the loops on the front of the rug. Be sure your yarn flows freely; the slightest tug on it will pull the stitches out or make them uneven.

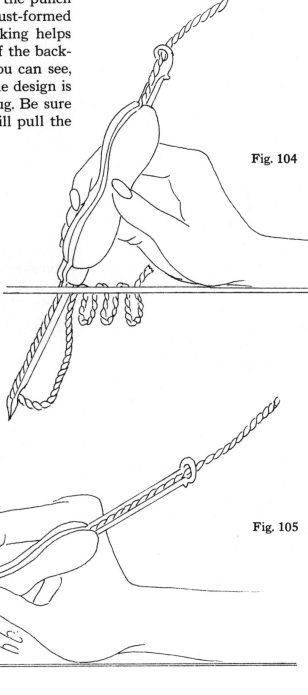

Fig. 104

Fig. 105

The spacing of the stitches varies with the height of the loop; in general, stitches with a short loop or thin yarn are made closer together than those with longer loops and thicker yarn.

A good stitch gauge is 24 to 30 stitches per square inch; work six rows to the inch and four or five stitches to each row, depending on the yarn and the height of the loop (see Fig. 106). There is no firm rule about placement of stitches. In general, try to space them to give a nice firm feel to the project, close enough together so none of the backing shows from the front yet not so crowded as to cause the loops to bunch up and the surface to bubble or ripple.

Loose ends should never be left on the back of the work where they can catch and easily unravel the newly formed stitches.

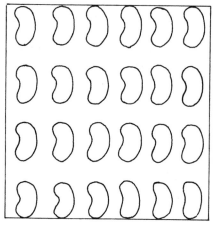

Fig. 106

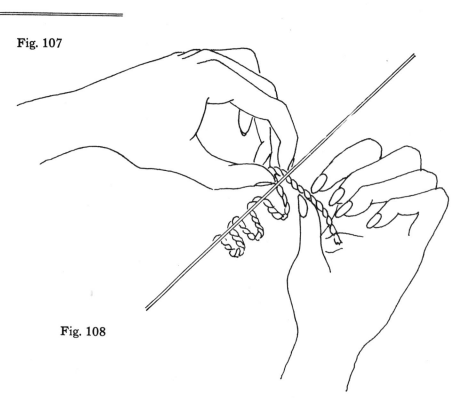

Fig. 107

As you can see from Fig. 107, a tail of yarn rests on the back of the work where you start to stitch. By pulling carefully on the first loop on the front of the project, you can pull this tail through the backing to the front of the work, where it will nestle inconspicuously among the already formed loops (see Fig. 108). Similarly, when you

Fig. 108

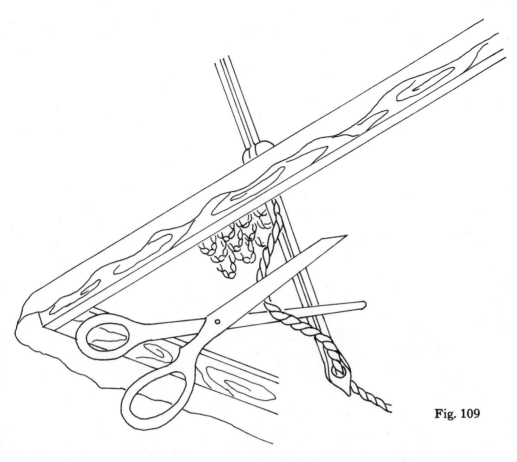

Fig. 109

finish stitching one area, cut the yarn on the front (the looped side) about halfway up the shaft of the needle when it is plunged into the backing (see Fig. 109); then withdraw the punch hook, leaving the cut yarn end at the front. If necessary, trim the cut ends so they are shorter than the loops that surround them (see Fig. 110).

Fig. 110

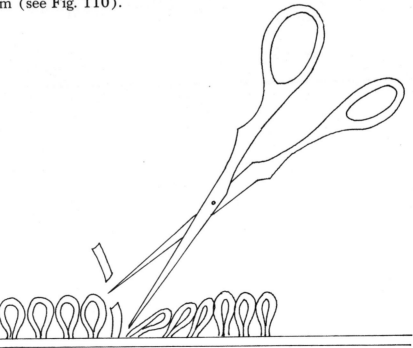

# WORKING THE DESIGN

Although there are no fixed ways of working the project, here is a good plan:

Stitch single lines and the smallest areas of color first, then move on to larger areas. Stitch the background last.

For each separate form or design, outline the area and then fill in the center. Make your rows of stitches parallel to the contours of the outline and work around and around toward the center (see Fig. 111).

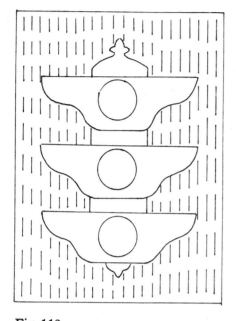

Fig. 112

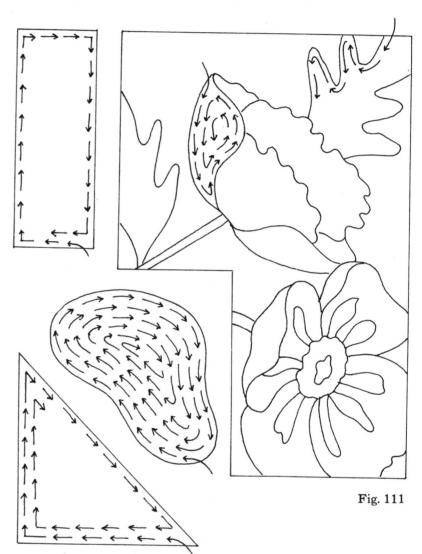

Fig. 111

Fig. 113

Background areas can be stitched in one or more of the following ways:

Straight lines, either horizontally or vertically punched, cover the area quickly and give a sharp clean look (see Fig. 112).

Curves, waves, circles, and semicircles add dynamic vitality and movement (see Fig. 113).

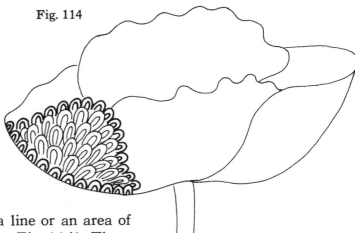

Fig. 114

## Stitching Hints and Reminders

*** If you want to emphasize a line or an area of the design, outline it with short loops (see Fig. 114). These will be buried among the higher loops but their presence provides just enough extra room to set off the designated area. If your punch hook cannot adjust for short enough loops, impale one or more rubber washers on the shaft of the needle to shorten the stitching stroke (see Fig. 115).

*** For additional emphasis you can outline a shape in one color and fill it in with another color. Or for a richer color effect, outline in one color and fill in with another shade of the same color.

*** Incorporate loops of varying heights in the same project for additional textural interest. For example, stitch the face of an animal in low loops and his body fur in longer loops.

*** In a rug, don't carry yarn from one area to another over any great distance since the raised yarn will receive greater wear.

*** To blend contiguous areas of color into each other, end rows in random lengths where they will be joined so that "fingers" of color protrude into the adjacent areas (see Fig. 116). This is also a good technique to use when you are making a project larger than your frame and have to join areas of stitching after you move the backing on the frame and retack it.

Fig. 115

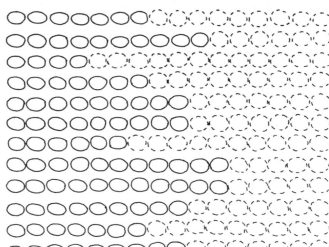

Fig. 116

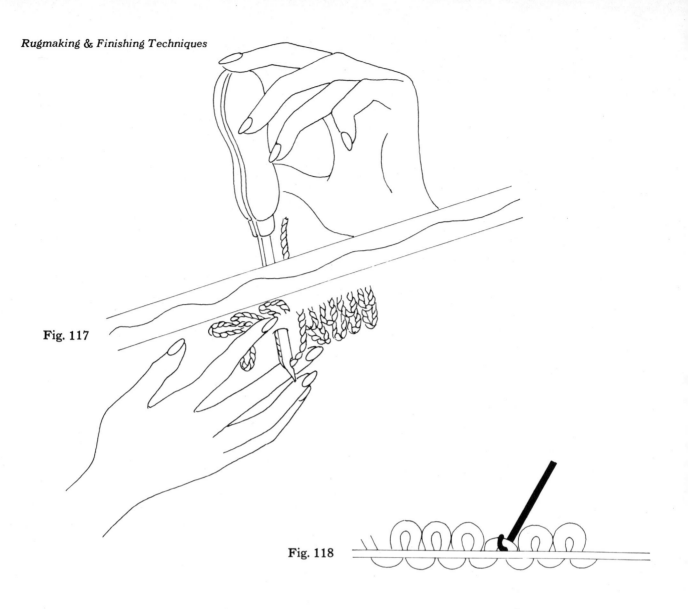

Fig. 117

Fig. 118

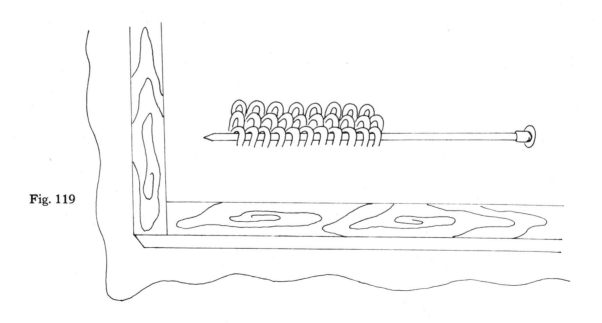

Fig. 119

## FINISHING THE RUG

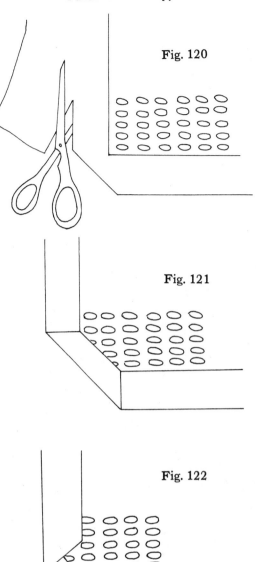

Fig. 120

Fig. 121

Fig. 122

After you have completed punching the design, check the looped side—the front of the project—to be sure that no unintended areas of the backing fabric show. If any unwanted spots are visible, insert additional stitches or rows, using a finer yarn if the areas to be filled are particularly small or narrow. To be sure that these added stitches don't become entangled in or split the already formed loops, separate them with your free hand as you punch (see Fig. 117).

At the same time check and repair any loops that might have loosened or slipped out of the backing. If one loop is shorter than its neighbors, use a crochet hook to pull it up to the proper height (see Fig. 118). If many loops are uneven, insert a knitting needle or long nail through all of them and pull on it to make them uniform in height (see Fig. 119).

If any stitches have actually slipped out, leaving a hole in the backing, scratch that part of the backing with your fingernail to restore the weave. Then repunch the lost stitches.

Finally, be sure that all the yarn ends are on the front of the project and that they are trimmed shorter than the loops surrounding them.

Once the workmanship has been checked and corrected to your satisfaction, you are ready to anchor the stitching permanently with a coating of latex. With the project still tacked to the frame, turn the looped (front) side face down and apply liquid latex to the back with a spatula or piece of stiff cardboard. Spread it in a thin coat, covering all the stitches evenly. If you have deliberately left some portions of the backing unstitched as a decorative feature of the design, *do not apply latex* to that unstitched area lest it seep through and discolor the backing material. Let the latex set overnight. You will find that the latex backing not only anchors and secures the stitching but provides a non-skid surface for rugs.

Note: Latex is sold in hardware and craft stores under such trade names as Griptex, or as Saf-T-Bak at Sears, Roebuck and Company.

After the latex has dried over the stitching, remove the project from the frame. Cut the excess backing material all around to provide a 2-inch-wide hem, and cut the corners to within an inch of the stitching (see Fig. 120).

To miter the corners, first turn back each diagonal corner (see Fig. 121). Turn the side hems in over the back of the project, pulling them tightly enough so the hem doesn't show from the front but not so tightly that it pulls up, preventing the rug from lying flat (see Fig. 122). Pin the mitered corner together (see Fig. 123). Fold under the

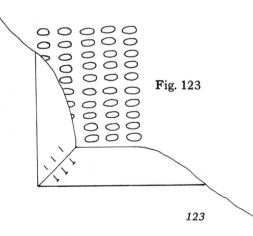

Fig. 123

raw edges, then pin each side hem to the back of the project (see Fig. 124). Apply liquid latex to the turned-in sides and corners. When the latex has almost but not completely dried, remove the pins. This additional coating of latex takes the place of sewing the hem.

On curved edges, make frequent small pleats to take up the slack as you go around the hem, and pin them to the backing (see Fig. 125). On angles or inside curves, you may have to slash the hem backing (see Fig. 126). Apply the liquid latex over the slashed and pinned hems as above.

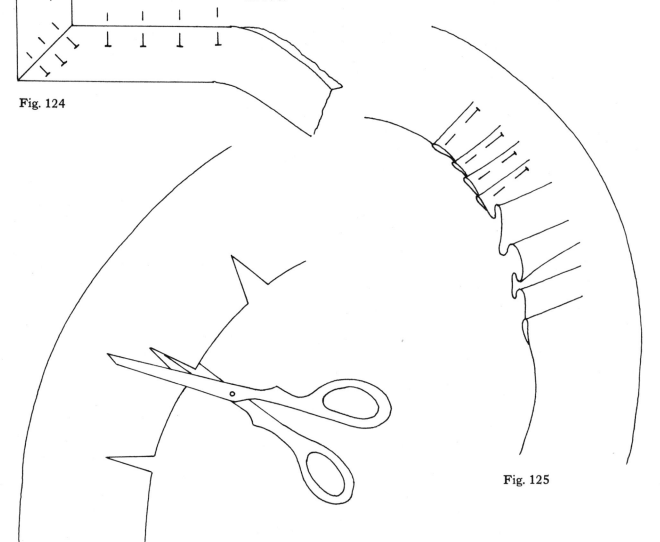

Fig. 124

Fig. 125

Fig. 126

\*\*\* If you find your finished rug or hanging curls up, roll it up with the looped side in for a time. Or lay it under a heavy rug for a few days.

\*\*\* After the loops have been locked in place by the latex coating, you can cut them for special textural effects as, for example, giving the lion a shaggy mane.

If you want a more elaborate finish or trim, or a lining, or want to display your rug as a wall hanging, see "Final Touches," next page, for more ideas.

# Final Touches

Your rug needs no further finishing other than that described under each rugmaking technique. However, you may want to line it, fringe or tassel it, or turn it into a wall hanging.

## LINING

For lining material choose a thin tightly woven fabric like cotton. Cut it an inch or two larger all around than the finished project. Lay the finished rug face down on a table or floor, and over it position the cut lining, face up. Pin the lining to the rug, wrong sides together, anchoring it in a few places in the center of the rug and in the middle of each side (see Fig. 127).

At each corner, turn back the lining and miter it to fit the rug (see Fig. 128). Pin each mitered lining corner in place, then turn under the side hems and pin in place. When the lining is entirely mitered and folded under on all sides,

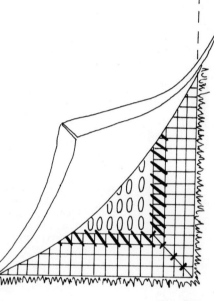

Fig. 128

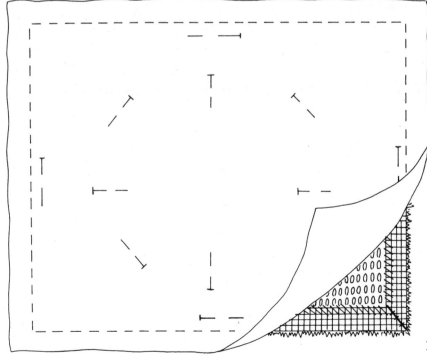

Fig. 127

blind stitch three sides of it to the back of the rug. On the bottom or fourth side neatly hem the lining without catching the back of the rug (see Fig. 129). You will be able to shake out any accumulations of dust or dirt through the open side.

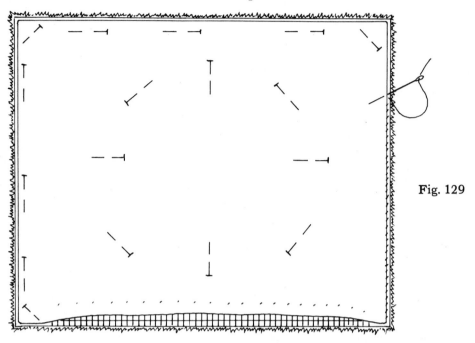

Fig. 129

### FRINGE BENEFITS

A fringe offers an attractive finish for almost any rug shape. Attach it all around a circular or square rug, or perhaps just at the two short ends of a rectangular one. The following fringes are equally useful with latch, needlepoint, or punch hooked rugs. They should all be attached before the lining.

*Commercial Fringe*

Ready-made fringes are available in many styles and colors at notions counters. Some of them are plain, some gathered in more elaborate configurations, others incorporate balls and other decorative features. Choose a fringe in keeping with the style and design of your rug, and pick up the color of the background or one of the design elements.

On all three types of rugs, blind stitch the fringe to the rug backing as close as you can to the rug stitches. On a punch rug, stitch it to the fabric backing (see Fig. 130). On latch rugs, stitch it to the binding. On needlepoint rugs, catch your needle around the threads of the canvas (see Fig. 131). When you turn a corner, make an inverted pleat in the fringe heading to take up the excess (see Fig. 132).

After you have securely anchored the fringe to the rug backing, line the rug as described above (see Fig. 133), still leaving the bottom or one side open.

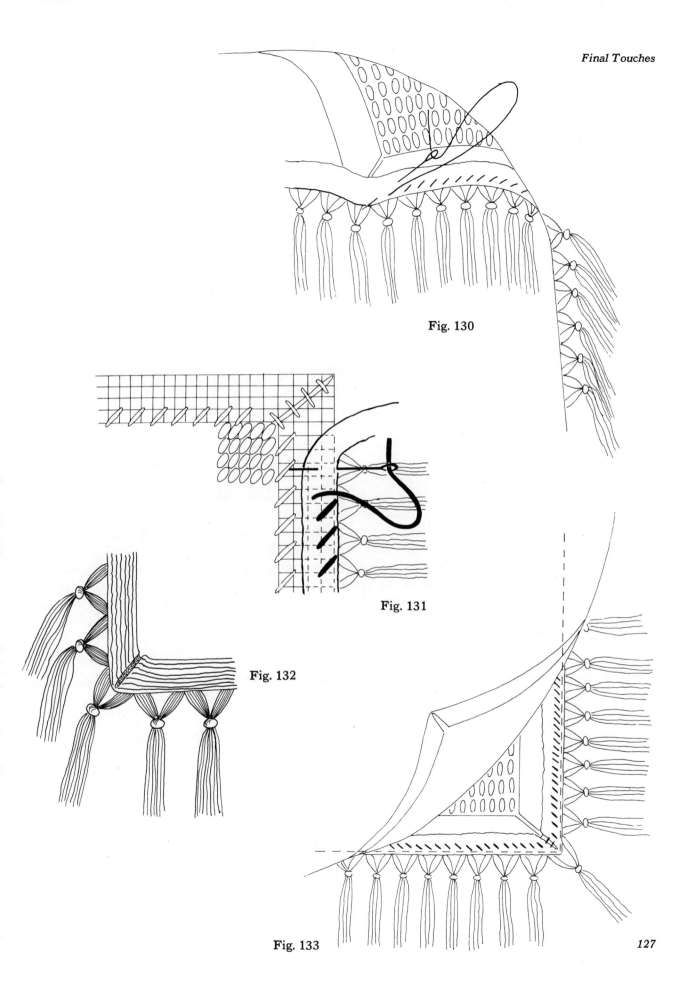

Final Touches

Fig. 130

Fig. 131

Fig. 132

Fig. 133

127

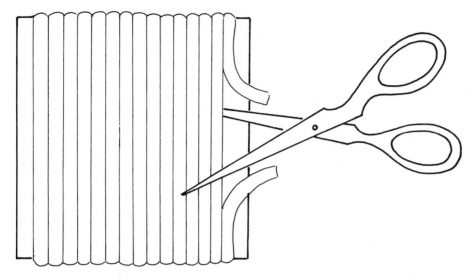

Fig. 134

## Custom Fringe Loops

Fringe made from the yarn used in the rug offers a custom finish not possible with a commercial fringe. You can make the fringe all one color from the background or a design element, or you can use any number of colors from the design, or even all of them.

The easiest kind of custom fringe to make is a simple loop for which you cut yarn into 8-inch lengths. You can do this easily by wrapping the yarn around a 4-inch-wide piece of cardboard and cutting it once (see Fig. 134).

To fringe a needlepoint or latched canvas, insert a crochet hook inside the outermost row of canvas thread at one corner of the rug (see Fig. 135). Fold one of the yarn lengths in half over the crochet hook (see Fig. 136) and

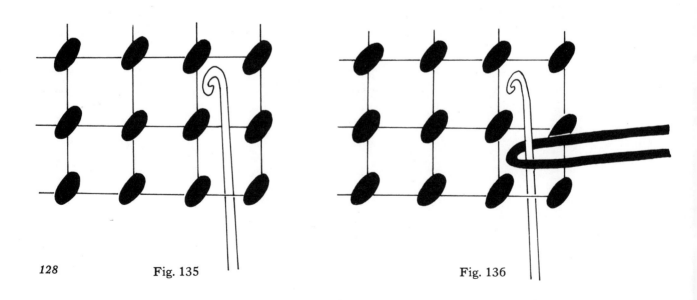

Fig. 135                                    Fig. 136

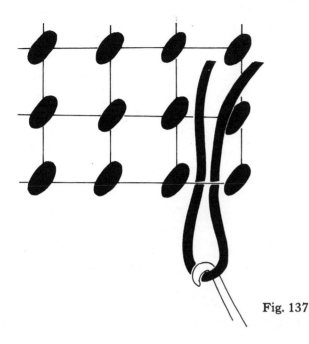

Fig. 137

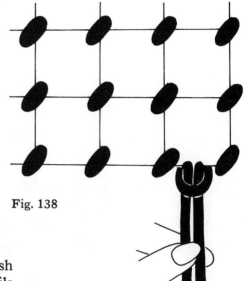

Fig. 138

pull the loop you have just formed through the canvas mesh about an inch (see Fig. 137). Now pull the two yarn tails through the loop, using the crochet hook or your fingers (see Fig. 138). Pull the tail ends to tighten the loop, making sure the two ends are even. In the same manner work across the side of the rug, inserting the fringing loops every quarter inch or so. If you want a thicker fringe, make the loops closer together, or use two or more lengths of yarn for a single loop. If you want a multi-colored fringe, combine two or more colors in one loop (see Fig. 139).

Note: If you are fringing adjacent sides of a rug, you will have to make a number of separate loops in the corner mesh in order to provide enough fullness (see Fig. 140).

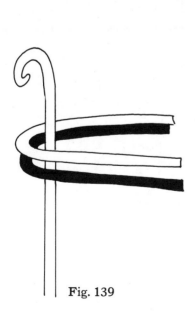

Fig. 139

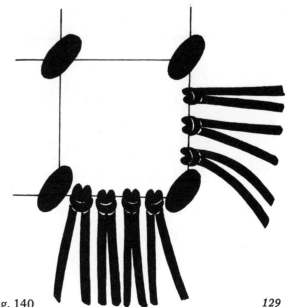

Fig. 140

*129*

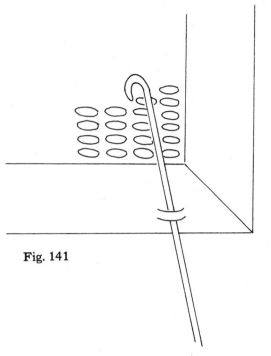

Fig. 141

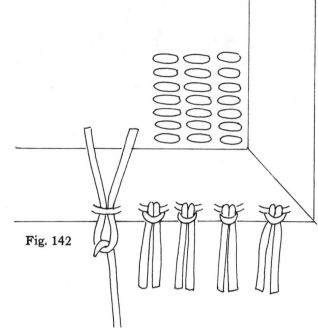

Fig. 142

To fringe a punch hooked rug made on a fairly loosely woven backing, insert the crochet hook through the hem about ¼ inch from the edge (see Fig. 141). Then form each looped fringe as described above (see Figs. 135-138), making them about ¼ inch apart (see Fig. 142).

If your fabric backing is too tightly woven to accommodate a crochet hook, make a row of stitches on which to hang the looped fringe, as follows:

Using a tapestry needle and a knotted strand of yarn, insert the needle into the hem at *1* (and at subsequent odd numbers) about an inch in from the edge of the hem; push the needle out at *2* (and at subsequent even numbers) about ½ inch in from the edge of the hem (see Fig. 143). Be sure to catch only the hem; your needle should not go through the face of the rug. As you pull the needle through the hem to complete a stitch, hold the preceding stitch behind the needle (see Fig. 144). Make a row

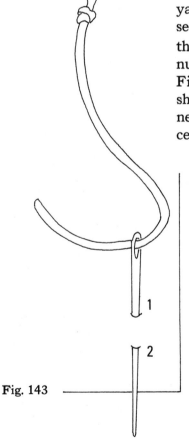

Fig. 143

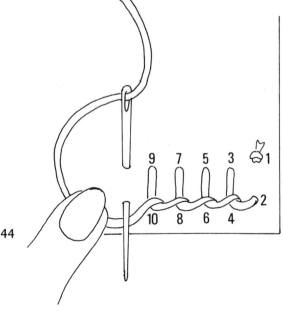

Fig. 144

of these anchoring stitches ¼ to ½ inch apart along the sides to be fringed, rotating the rug 90 degrees when turning a corner (see Fig. 145).

To complete the fringing, fold the prepared lengths of yarn over the crochet hook and form the loops as described above. Make one or more loops per stitch, as required for thickness of fringing, especially at the corners (see Fig. 146).

If you want to line your rug, follow the instructions given in the beginning of this chapter and see Figs. 127-129.

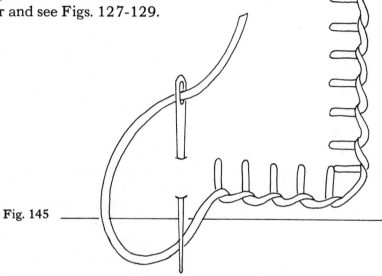

Fig. 145

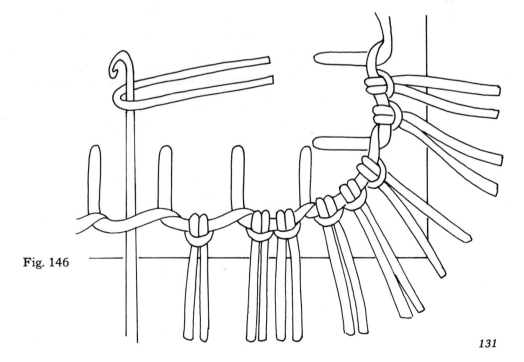

Fig. 146

# TURN YOUR RUG INTO A WALL HANGING

Pride of accomplishment often prompts craftsmen to display their rugs on the wall rather than underfoot. The principal item you need to turn a rug into a wall hanging is a wooden mounting board about 1½ to 2 inches wide, 2 inches shorter in length than the top of the hanging, and about ½ inch thick. The rug is attached to this board by Velcro or by tacks.

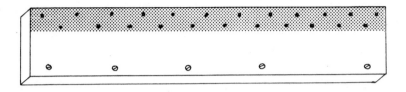

**Fig. 147**

**Fig. 148**

## Velcro Method

Continuous lengths of Velcro, a two-part nylon fastener, are available on a reel in a ¾-inch width. Cut the double Velcro strips the length of the mounting board. Place the "receiving" hook strip flush with the top of the mounting board, and staple or nail it with ⅜-inch tacks or any nails that won't penetrate the thickness of the board. Then nail or screw the board to the wall, placing these longer nails along the bottom edge of the board (see Fig. 147).

Sew the "attaching" loop strip of Velcro to the back of the wall hanging about ¼ inch down from the top edge (see Fig. 148). Press the top of the hanging to the mounting board to secure it in position (see Fig, 149).

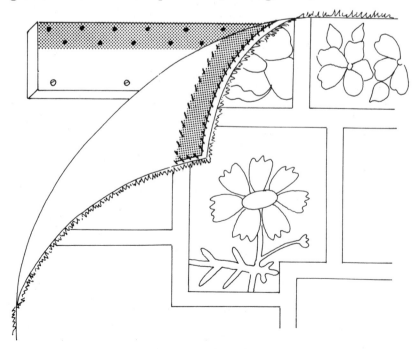

Fig. 149

## Tacking Method

Through the mounting board drive ¾-inch nails from the back to the front at an upward angle, setting them about 6 inches apart (see Fig. 150). If you are using a board of another thickness, use nails about ¼ inch longer than the thickness of the board. Nail or screw the board to the wall. Center the hanging over the mounting board and impale it on the protruding points of the nails, adjusting it until it lies straight (see Fig. 151). The nail points will be buried in the rug backing and the stitching.

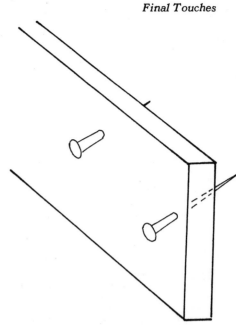

Fig. 150

Fig. 151

# *Where to Get What You Need*

Rugmaking supplies are probably available in or near your home town. You are likely to find them in craft and hobby shops, in the art needlework section of department stores, in five-and-ten-cent stores. Local outlets are preferable to mail order sources, not only for their convenience, but for their display of yarns and other rugmaking needs, their continuing instruction, and their encouragement, especially for beginners. However, if you can't find a suitable source in your area, here are some mail order suppliers listed alphabetically by state and city:

### ALABAMA

The Needleworks, 2906 Linden Avenue, Birmingham, Ala. 35209. *Needlepoint, latch.*

### ARIZONA

The Needlepoint Nook, 5037 North Seventh Avenue, Phoenix, Ariz. 85013. *Needlepoint.*

Busy Work Needlepoint Studios, Inc., P.O. Box 609, Scottsdale, Ariz. 85252. *Needlepoint.*

### CALIFORNIA

Haystack, Ltd., 240 South Beverly Drive, Beverly Hills, Calif. 90212. *Needlepoint.*

Port o'Call, 11965 San Vicente, Brentwood, Calif. 94513.

The Nimble Thimble, 911 Capitola Avenue East, Capitola, Calif. 95010. *Needlepoint, latch.*

Dorothy Lawless Rug Studio, 4501 Valdina Place, Los Angeles, Calif. 90043. *Punch hooking supplies.*

Petit Point Junction, 373 North Robertson Boulevard, Los Angeles, Calif. 90048. *Needlepoint, latch.*

Lazy Daisy Needlecraft Shop, 602 East Walnut Street, Pasadena, Calif. 91101. *Needlepoint, latch.*

Nimble Needle, 2645 San Diego Avenue, San Diego, Calif. 92110. *Needlepoint.*

The Knittery, 2040 Union Street, San Francisco, Calif. 94123. *Needlepoint.*

The Yarn Depot, 545 Sutter Street, San Francisco, Calif. 94102. *Rug yarns.*

The Needlecraft Shop, 4501 Van Nuys Boulevard, Sherman Oaks, Calif. 91403. *Needlepoint, latch, punch.*

## COLORADO

The Yarn Garden, Williams Village Shopping Center, 651 30th Street, Boulder, Colo. 80302. *Needlepoint.*

Golden Needle, 2356 East Third Avenue, Denver, Colo. 80206. *Needlepoint.*

The Point, 755 South Colorado Boulevard, Denver, Colo. 80222. *Needlepoint.*

## CONNECTICUT

The Designing Woman, Lakeville, Conn. 06039. *Needlepoint.*

Harry M. Fraser Co., 192 Hartford Road, Manchester, Conn. 06040. *Punch hooking.*

The Yarnbee, 413 Main Street, Ridgefield, Conn. 06877.

Pfistner Associates, 185 Frederick Street, Torrington, Conn. 06790. *Punch hooks.*

The Daisy, 998 Farmington Avenue, West Hartford, Conn. 06107. *Needlepoint, latch.*

## DELAWARE

Colonial Yarn Shop, Inc., 3930 Kennett Pike, Wilmington, Del. 19807.

## DISTRICT OF COLUMBIA

American Needlework Center, Inc., 2803 M Street, N.W., Washington, D.C. 20007.

The Elegant Needle, 5430 MacArthur Boulevard, N.W., Washington, D.C. 20016. *Needlepoint.*

## FLORIDA

Yarns Galore, Ponce de Leon Boulevard, Coral Gables, Fla. 33134. *Needlepoint.*

The Needlework Studio, P.O. Box 1754, Pompano Beach, Fla. 33061. *Needlepoint.*

Needle Nook, 6488 Central Avenue, St. Petersburg, Fla. 33707.

## GEORGIA

Papillon, Cates Plaza, 375 Pharr Road, N.E., Atlanta, Ga. 30305. *Needlepoint.*

Felker Art-Needlework Inc., 640 Valleybrook Road, Decatur, Ga. 30033.

## ILLINOIS

Needlepoint Works, Inc., 1660 North La Salle Street, Chicago, Ill. 60614.

Nimble Needles, 340 West Armitage Avenue, Chicago, Ill. 60614.

Nina Needlepoint, 120 East Delaware Place, Chicago, Ill. 60611.

LeeWards, Elgin, Ill. 60120.

Norden Products, Glenview, Ill. 60025. *Punch.*

Magic Needle, 44 Green Bay Road, Winnetka, Ill. 60093.

## INDIANA

Craft Kaleidoscope, 6412 Ferguson Street, Indianapolis, Ind. 46220.

Town Stitchery, 6516 Cornell Avenue, Indianapolis, Ind. 46220.

## LOUISIANA

The Quarter Stitch, 532 St. Peter Street, New Orleans, La. 70130. *Needlepoint.*

## MARYLAND

Needlecraft Shop, Yorktowne Plaza Shopping Center, Baltimore, Md. 21030.

Craft Kit and Caboodle, 10400 Old Georgetown Road, Bethesda, Md. 20314.

The Needlecraft Center, 1079 Rockville Pike, Rockville, Md. 20852.

## MASSACHUSETTS

Nimble Fingers, Inc., 37 Newbury Street, Boston, Mass. 02116. *Needlepoint, latch.*

Nantucket Needleworks, 11 South Water Street, Nantucket Island, Mass. 02554. *Needlepoint.*

Needlecraft House, West Townsend, Mass. 01474. *Needlepoint.*

## MICHIGAN

Needlepoint a la Carte, 325 South Woodward, Birmingham, Mich. 48011. *Needlepoint, latch.*

Peacock Alley, 650 Croswell Street, S.E., Grand Rapids, Mich. 49506. *Needlepoint.*

## MINNESOTA

The Jeweled Needle, 1009 Nicollet Avenue, Minneapolis, Minn. 55403. *Needlepoint.*

Needlework Unlimited, Inc., 5028 Frace Avenue South, Minneapolis, Minn. 55410. *Needlepoint, latch.*

## MISSOURI

In Stitches, 421 Nichols Road, Kansas City, Mo. 64112. *Needlepoint.*

The Studio, 316 West 63 Street, Kansas City, Mo. 64113. *Needlepoint.*

Krick Kits, 31 North Brentwood Boulevard, St. Louis, Mo. 63105. *Needlepoint.*

Wilson Brothers Mfg. Co., Route 8, Box 33-H, Springfield, Mo. 65804. *Punch.*

## NEW HAMPSHIRE

The Dorr Mill Store, Guild, N.H. 03754. *Punch hooking.*

## NEW YORK

The Knitting Needle, 2A McDonald Avenue, Armonk, N.Y. 10504. *Needlepoint, latch.*

T. E. Doelger, Box 126, Blauvelt, N.Y. 10913. *Needlepoint.*

Niddy Noddy, 416 Albany Post Road, Croton-on-Hudson, N.Y. 10520. *Rug yarns.*

Hilde's Knit Shop, 315 White Plains Post Road, Eastchester, N.Y. 10709. *Needlepoint, latch.*

George Wells Rugs, Inc., 565 Cedar Swamp Road, Glen Head, N.Y. 11545. *Punch hooking.*

Eye of the Needle, 157 Larchmont Avenue, Larchmont, N.Y. 10538. *Needlepoint.*

Needleworks of Larchmont, 136 Chatsworth Avenue, Larchmont, N.Y. 10538. *Needlepoint, latch.*

Boutique Margot, 26 West 54 Street, New York, N.Y. 10019. *Needlepoint.*

Coulter Studios, Inc., 118 East 59 Street, New York, N.Y. 10022. *Needlepoint, latch, punch.*

Alice Maynard, 724 Fifth Avenue, New York, N.Y. 10019. *Needlepoint, latch, punch.*

Nina Needlepoint, 860 Madison Avenue, New York, N.Y. 10021. *Needlepoint.*

Paternayan Bros., Inc., 312 East 95 Street, New York, N.Y. 10028. *Punch: rug backings of Duraback and monk's cloth.*

Selma's Art Needlework, 1645 Second Avenue, New York, N.Y. 10028. *Needlepoint, latch.*

Erica Wilson, Inc., 717 Madison Avenue, New York, N.Y. 10021. *Needlepoint.*

Black Sheep, 48 Purchase Street, Rye, N.Y. 10580. *Needlepoint, latch.*

Knitting Studio, 78 Purchase Street, Rye, N.Y. 10580. *Latch.*

Handy Lady, 72 Garth Road, Scarsdale, N.Y. 10583. *Needlepoint, latch.*

## PENNSYLVANIA

Sophisti-Kits, P.O. Box 5020, Pittsburgh, Pa. 15206. *Needlepoint.*

Sinkler Needlepoint Studio, 223 Iven Avenue, Box 93, Radnor, Pa. 19087. *Needlepoint.*

## RHODE ISLAND

Needlecraft Nook, 22 Child Street, Warren, R.I. 02885. *Latch.*

## TENNESSEE

Canvas Patch Originals, P.O. Box 3072, Oak Ridge, Tenn. 37830. *Needlepoint.*

## TEXAS

Needle Art Boutique, 2800 Routh Street, Dallas, Texas 75201.

Needlework Patio, 6925 Snider Plaza, Dallas, Texas 75205.

## VIRGINIA

Yarn Bazaar, 421 South Washington Street, Alexandria, Va. 22314.

Yarns Etcetera, 215 King Street, Alexandria, Va. 22314.

Needlework Nook, 431 Forest Avenue, Richmond, Va. 23223.

## WASHINGTON

The Needle Works, 4518 39th Place, N.E., Seattle, Wash. 98105.

The large mail order houses like Sears, Roebuck and Co. also carry a wide variety of rugmaking supplies.

Copying pencils for the hot iron transfer method are available from:

Boutique Margot, 26 West 54 Street, New York, N.Y. 10019.

The Dorr Mill Store, Guild, N.H. 03754.

George Wells Rugs, Inc., 565 Cedar Swamp Road, Glen Head, N.Y. 11545.